A Second Home

PROJECT SPONSORS

Missouri Center for the Book
Western Historical Manuscript Collection
    University of Missouri–Columbia

Special Thanks

Jeanelle Ash, Curator, Ralph Foster Museum, College of the Ozarks
Marilyn France, editor, *White River Valley Historical Quarterly*
Christine Montgomery, State Historical Society of Missouri, Columbia
Claudia Powell, Western Historical Manuscript Collection, University
    of Missouri–Columbia
John Viessman, Museum Curator, Missouri Department of Natural
    Resources

MISSOURI HERITAGE READERS
General Editor, Rebecca B. Schroeder

Each Missouri Heritage Reader explores a particular aspect of the state's rich cultural heritage. Focusing on people, places, historical events, and the details of daily life, these books illustrate the ways in which people from all parts of the world contributed to the development of the state and the region. The books incorporate documentary and oral history, folklore, and informal literature in a way that makes these resources accessible to all Missourians.

Intended primarily for adult new readers, these books will also be invaluable to readers of all ages interested in the cultural and social history of Missouri.

Other Books in the Series

A Second Home

Missouri's Early Schools

Sue Thomas

UNIVERSITY OF MISSOURI PRESS
COLUMBIA AND LONDON

Library of Congress Cataloging-in-Publication Data

Thomas, Sue, 1932–
   A second home : Missouri's early schools / Sue Thomas.
      p. cm. — (Missouri heritage readers)
   Summary: "History of early schools in Missouri, including accounts of teach-
ing materials and methods and schoolday activities. Describes schools in fron-
tier settlements such as Ste. Genevieve. Discusses the beginnings of public
education in the 1850s and the contributions of John Berry Meachum, James
Milton Turner, and other African American leaders"—Provided by publisher.
   Includes bibliographical references and index.
   ISBN-13: 978-0-8262-1669-4 (pbk. : alk. paper)
   ISBN-10: 0-8262-1669-2 (pbk. : alk. paper)
   1. Education—Missouri—History. 2. Schools—Missouri—History. I. Title.
II. Series.
   LA316.T46 2006
370'.977809—dc22

                                                            2006010059

   ∞™ This paper meets the requirements of the
American National Standard for Permanence of Paper
   for Printed Library Materials, Z39.48, 1984.

Designer: Stephanie Foley
Typesetter: foleydesign
Printer and binder: Thomson-Shore, Inc.
Typefaces: Goudy and Ramona

This book is dedicated to my granddaughter,
Elisabeth Hawley, who studies readin',
'ritin', and 'rithmetic each day in school.

Contents

Acknowledgments

My thanks to the following teachers, former students, and historians who took the time to locate information about early schools and to welcome me into their homes:

Boonville: Adolph Hilden; Buffalo: Thelma Kurtz; Bunceton: Jeanette Heaton; California: Thelma Hines Sappington, Richard Schroeder; Columbia: Mrs. Joe (Lucy) Douglas, Marion Terrell Shaw, Rebecca B. Schroeder; Dunnegan: Jerrie Lynch; Eminence: Edna Staples; Fulton: Bill Hamilton; Hermann: Gennie Tesson; Holt: Jean Everling, Gail Goeke; Holts Summit: John and Betty Jo McKim; Houston: Alice Crawford, Pauline Young, Ruth Massey, Audrey Bandy, Mary Jane Medders, Mildred Melton; Jefferson City: Jim Morris, Regina Robinson, Nancy Ogg, Jeanette de la Torre, Patt Behler, Madeline Matson; Kansas City: Bill Livingston, Mary Beveridge; Koshkonong: Mildred McCormack; Lathrop: Gerald Snodgrass; Montgomery City: Marjorie Miller; Mountain Grove: Vearl Rowe; New Franklin: Thelma Sappington; Overland Park, Kansas: Betty Collum Harrison; Paris: Louis Yusko, Lou B. Callis, Zelma Menefee; Plattsburg: Avanelle Dedman, Karma Kay, Gladys Handley; Preston: Hoyt and Margaret Owsley; Sedalia: Linda McCollum; Stockton: Anna Lee Lower; Tipton: Della Huff; Vienna: Jean Henderson, Mozelle Hutchison, Mrs. Carl Baldwin; Watkins Mill: Plora Walby; Webb City: Ralph L. Hooker.

*

Thanks also to staff members of the following libraries and archives for answering questions and providing historical information: Black Archives of Mid-America; Clay County Archives and Historical Library; Inman E. Page Library, Lincoln University; Jackson County Archives and Library; Missouri Department of Natural Resources; Missouri State Archives; Missouri Supreme Court Library; Missouri Valley Special Collections–Kansas City Public Library; State Historical Society of Missouri, Columbia; Western Historical Manuscript Collection–Columbia; Western Historical Manuscript Collection–Kansas City; Western Historical Manuscript Collection–St. Louis; Walters–Boone County Historical Museum.

A Second Home

Introduction

Children on the Frontier

C hildren arriving in St. Louis in the early 1800s found strange sights and sounds everywhere in the small settlement on the west bank of the Mississippi River. Parents and children alike must have been amazed at the colorful crowds: a fur trader standing on the riverbank with his hair pulled back in a braid (known as a queue) and wearing leather pants with pouches and knives hanging from his belt; an Osage woman with the part in her hair painted red to symbolize the path of the sun across the sky; French women clattering to market in wooden shoes, wearing traditional white caps and white aprons over colorful dresses; and slaves and black boat hands in brightly colored bandannas chanting in French while loading keelboats from the levee. Families from the settled eastern states encountered French and Spanish merchants and fur traders, slaves and free blacks, and Native Americans of many different tribes in this early frontier settlement of what is now Missouri.

French settlers had established Ste. Genevieve, the first permanent European settlement in Missouri, about 1750. By 1772 it was the largest settlement in the territory with 691 residents, including 287 slaves. The population of St. Louis at the time was 597, which included 198 slaves. The French observer Nicolas de Finiels, who spent a year in St. Louis in the late 1790s and explored settlements in the area, found the people of Ste. Genevieve and the nearby settlement of New Bourbon "simply an extended family. . . . Their pains are endured together; they

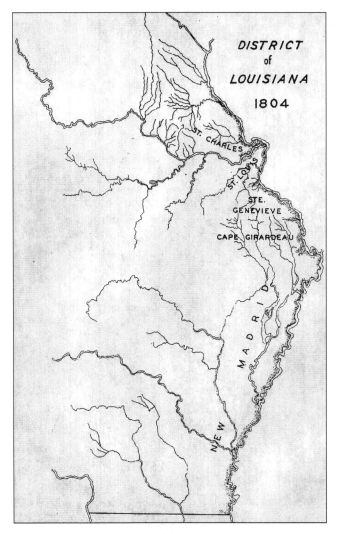

Before the Louisiana Purchase, travelers visiting the area that is now Missouri knew it by many names: Upper Louisiana, Spanish Illinois, and the Illinois Country, among others. When the United States took possession of the Louisiana Territory from France in 1804, only a few settlements existed in the upper part of the territory, scattered along the Mississippi River from New Madrid to St. Louis and St. Charles. Various Native American tribes lived or hunted there. By the 1840s emigrating pioneers from the east had expanded settlement westward to the state line with Kansas Territory. (State Historical Society of Missouri, Columbia)

are shared and . . . easier to endure. Likewise their pleasures belong to everyone."

Others did not view Ste. Genevieve as favorably as did Finiels. Perrin du Lac, a Frenchman visiting the village in 1802, found young people spending their time riding, hunting, and dancing. He described the children as being "raised pell-mell with the little savages" and "without schooling and with no desire to acquire it." But Finiels, a more sympathetic observer, praised "the sweet harmony" of the villagers. "I cannot leave Ste. Genevieve without rendering homage to its residents, a tribute, I hope, that every visitor will pay them for a long time to come."

In 1764, New Orleans trader Pierre de Laclède Liguest and his stepson, fourteen-year-old Auguste Chouteau, founded the settlement upriver from Ste. Genevieve that became St. Louis. Laclède had sent his young stepson and a party of workers from Kaskaskia, Illinois, where they had spent the winter, to clear the location for a trading post. On the morning of February 15, 1764, the boy cut the first tree to build the post on the site that Laclède predicted would be a great city of the future. He named the settlement for Louis IX, the crusader king and patron saint of Louis XV, the reigning king of France, not knowing that the Louisiana Territory had been transferred to Spain in 1762.

Auguste Chouteau, like many other children at the time, began to work as soon as he was old enough to be useful. There was a great shortage of labor on the new frontier, and children were valuable as workers. Records show that Auguste, himself only fourteen, had two twelve-year-olds and another fourteen-year-old on his work crew to build the isolated trading post. For the majority of families in pioneer days, the labor of every adult and every child was necessary to accomplish the goal of building for a better future.

French merchants in St. Louis were successful in their early efforts to establish trade with the Indians. By 1769, according to Charles van Ravenswaay's *St. Louis: An Informal History*, twenty-five or more tribes from both sides of the Mississippi River visited St. Louis each year, usually in May or June. "They held councils with the French, traded their furs, feasted, and received gifts at the expense of the Spanish king." Although France had

ceded the Louisiana Territory to Spain, French traders and settlers continued to move across the Mississippi, preferring the
rule of the Spanish to that of the British, who had held the
Illinois Country east of the river since the end of the French and
Indian War in the 1760s. By 1780, St. Louis was three blocks
wide and spread out along the Mississippi River.

After the United States purchased the Louisiana Territory
from France in 1803, both American and European immigrants
started to pour into the new area to claim lands and establish
homes. Charles van Ravenswaay reported that by the 1820s St.
Louis had become a "pageant of nationalities, each with its own
characteristic dress." He described "black women in crisp,
bright-colored garments and carefully arranged turbans" and
many other residents dressed in colorful costumes. In addition
to the Creoles, Native Americans, and Africans, Old Stock
American pioneers arriving in St. Louis found Italians, Poles,
Germans, Swiss, French, English, Irish, and Dutch, all seeking
their fortunes in the "Far West."

Jesse Benton Frémont, the daughter of Thomas Hart Benton,
one of Missouri's first two senators, wrote many years later of her
childhood in St. Louis in the 1830s.

> St. Louis was not more than a *petite ville* in numbers, yet . . .
> it had a stirring life. . . . The governing religion was of
> course Catholic as this had been so lately a French posses-
> sion and its chief people were the French settlers who were
> also the chief traders in furs. Priests and Sisters of Charity
> in their special black dress were everywhere in the streets,
> so were the army officers in service-worn uniforms, and the
> French peasant women wore, as in France, their thick
> white caps, sabots [wooden shoes] and full red petticoats
> with big blue or yellow handkerchiefs crossed over the
> white bodices; and with the Indians painted and blanketed
> gliding along in files . . . one would have been puzzled to
> say whose country it was now.

This lively St. Louis settlement was on the border of an
immense and almost unexplored Indian country. The Missouri,

Osage, Shawnee, Kaskaskia, Ponca, Tamaroa, Mascoutah, Utz, Delaware, Sioux, Ioway, Sac, Fox, Illini, Potawatomi, and Kickapoo Indians roamed freely in the lands west of St. Louis, setting up their camps in fields of wild grasses, along the many streams, or on hillsides thickly covered with cedar.

Natalie Hesse, who came from Germany to Missouri in 1835 with her family, described in her diary the Indians she saw:

> We children ran to look at the men who were so strange to us. They had covered themselves in large woolen blankets and their faces and arms were painted with all kinds of flowers and their heads were decorated with colorful feathers. Some had shaved their heads bald and in the middle of them they had a tuft of hair; . . . others were wearing rings around their knees which were decorated with bells all around, of which they seemed to be terribly proud for they frequently looked at them with great pleasure. One German gave them a flintstone and tinder [for starting a fire] and showed them how to use these things. One could see the joy they felt by looking at their faces.

Pioneers from the east or from Europe usually set out west from St. Louis by land, in wagons or on foot, eager to find "congressional land" to claim. By 1850, when the population of Missouri had grown to 650,000, the great western movement had made its way to the state's western boundary, where the Santa Fe Trail trade with Mexico brought its own sights and sounds to emigrants going farther west. In *The Oregon Trail*, Francis J. Parkman wrote of his 1846 journey:

> We began to see signs of the great western movement that was taking place. Parties of emigrants, with their tents and wagons, were encamped on open spots near the bank . . . . On a rainy day, near sunset, we reached the landing . . . which is some miles from the river, on the extreme frontier of Missouri. The scene was characteristic, for here were represented at one view the most remarkable features of this wild and enterprising region. On the muddy shore stood

some thirty or forty dark . . . Spaniards, gazing . . . out from beneath their broad hats. They were attached to one of the Santa Fé companies, whose wagons were crowded together on the banks above. In the midst of these, crouching over a smoldering fire, was a group of Indians, belonging to a remote Mexican tribe. One or two French hunters from the mountains, with their long hair and buckskin dresses were looking at the boat; and seated on a log close at hand were three men, with rifles lying across their knees. The foremost of these, a tall, strong figure, with a clear blue eye and an open, intelligent face, might very well represent that race of restless and intrepid pioneers whose axes and rifles have opened a path from the Alleghenies to the western prairies.

And what of the pioneer children? In *Settlers' Children*, Elizabeth Hampsten describes their lives:

> These settlement childhoods were not easy. Many parents said that they came west "for the children" following the script of the American dream. They wanted to assure their children better economic and social opportunities than they themselves had had. . . . [But] in the first years of settlement, what was done "for" the children often caused them severe hardship. . . . Work, not play, was what children "did."

Their new life in the unknown territory of Missouri did introduce these children to the "strange ways" of others in a strange land. This was often exciting, but sometimes it was frightening. Whether traveling in a covered wagon (and sometimes seeing Indians standing in a silent row on the bluff above), walking through prairie grass so tall they could not see over it, or riding on a steamboat meeting strangers, children, along with their parents, gained a knowledge of the land, its people, and their surroundings. Each day the once-new sights and sounds became a more natural part of their daily lives.

Chapter One

The First Schools in Upper Louisiana

Limited educational opportunities in Upper Louisiana during the Spanish period placed even the most rudimentary education beyond the reach of the average child in the province.

— William E. Foley, A History of Missouri, Volume I, 1672 to 1820

Many French settlers in the Upper Louisiana Territory—also known then as "the Illinois Country," "Spanish Illinois," or "Spanish Louisiana"—did not read or write. In France, working people learned through apprenticeships, a practice that continued in this new world. Formal schooling was considered of little value to children expected to work in lead and salt mines. They needed more practical skills to survive. Some French immigrants, migrating to the Mississippi valley from Canada, had barely enough money to pay ferriage across the rivers. Work took priority over schooling for their children.

The few wealthy and well-educated French living in St. Louis, Ste. Genevieve, and New Bourbon owned books covering a variety of topics—history, science, literature, travel, and geography. Pierre Laclède Liguest, cofounder of St. Louis with his stepson Auguste Chouteau, had 150 books in his library. But libraries were a luxury of the wealthy, and rather than starting schools, wealthy French families in the early settlements often either engaged tutors or sent their children to schools in Canada or France.

French families of Ste. Genevieve lived near one another in the village, cultivating their crops in a common field outside the village. Travelers reported that children were included in the frequent entertainments in the homes of village leaders. The French preserved many traditional celebrations, such as dancing from home to home on New Year's Eve, singing a begging song and collecting food for a holiday feast. (State Historical Society of Missouri, Columbia)

While the Spanish governed the territory from 1762 to 1800, their primary interest was in the natural resources of the region. They neglected to develop any general educational system. However, individuals made some efforts in several villages and settlements. Jean Baptiste Truteau, a fur trader, opened the first small private tuition school in a log cabin in St. Louis in 1774, operating it off and on until about 1827. A Madame Maria Josepha Pinconneau *dit* Rigauche opened a school for girls in St. Louis in 1797. Governor Francisco de Carondelet, the Spanish administrator in New Orleans, had promised to send Madame Rigauche a monthly stipend to provide for the school; he failed to keep his promise, but she finally secured a land grant in 1800.

Several educated residents of Ste. Genevieve tried schools in the village during the years of Spanish rule. The few early schools were coeducational, but most often the village was without a school or teacher. Augustin-Charles Frémon de Laurière, who had immigrated to America when he lost most of his fortune in the French Revolution, developed one of the most ambitious educational programs there. In 1795, at the request of Pierre Delassus de Luzières, he worked out a careful plan of study and opened his school. In "Frontier Education in Spanish Louisiana," published in the *Missouri Historical Review* in April 1941, Ernest R. Liljegren describes Frémon's methods. He based the classes on a French theory of education developed by Louis-René de la Chalotais, which stressed practical education. It was designed to prepare students to earn a living and included the study of the principles of agriculture. It also focused on proper social manners, family values, and patriotism. Students were encouraged to write about their occupations, their amusements, or their troubles. Chalotais's theory, as summarized by Frémon, was that "education is a point so essential and so important that upon it alone depends quite generally the destiny of our life. A good education gives us the necessary forces to sustain adversities. . . . It enlightens us in the true principles of virtue and the true philosophy; and [teaches] that it is necessary besides to detest wrong and love good." According to Carl J. Ekberg, the school in Ste. Genevieve continued for at least two years. Ekberg found no evidence that it was coeducational, but since earlier schools in the village were, he believes Frémon must have accepted girls.

Henry Marie Brackenridge lived with a French family in Ste. Genevieve in the 1790s and wrote about his experiences many years later. His father sent him to Missouri from Pittsburgh when he was seven years old to learn French, believing, as Brackenridge wrote, that "a man doubles himself by learning another language." The boy arrived knowing two words of French, "oui" and "non," yes and no, but the French children in the village were kind to him, and he soon learned to speak the language. Brackenridge believed that the dances, much criticized by Americans, served as "schools for manners, in which the children of the rich and poor were placed on a footing of absolute equality" and that the "secret of true politeness, self-denial, or the giving of the better place to others, was taught at

Although in 1788 Colonel George Morgan developed a detailed plan to establish New Madrid as the first American settlement west of the Mississippi, the Spanish government rejected most of his proposals. The six schools he planned were never built. The town he named remained primarily a settlement of Canadian fur traders and trappers until after the Louisiana Purchase, when population began to increase. But these early American settlers evidently valued education. Lynn Morrow discovered a list of toasts given at a public dinner on July 4, 1806, which he published in "New Madrid and Its Hinterland, 1783–1826." Toast number 14 was "to education . . . those who desire a continuation of it must not neglect the establishment of schools." (State Historical Society of Missouri, Columbia)

these little balls." He also learned skills from the Indian boys near the village, such as how to shoot a bow and arrow and some of their language.

French engineer Nicolas de Finiels, on his visit to the area toward the end of the Spanish Colonial period in the late 1790s, described the amusements that young Brackenridge must have enjoyed in Ste. Genevieve. "In Ste. Genevieve people often gather in the homes of the commandant or other important residents. Everyone is welcome at these affairs provided you have a good reputation. Sometimes there is dancing, but more often they play games that everyone enjoys. The more comical the better, for laughter and gaiety are what they usually enjoy most."

As early as 1788, Colonel George Morgan, a land speculator who had the support of the Spanish minister to the United States, was planning the first "American" town west of the Mississippi. He circulated handbills and recruited settlers to a location he had selected on the west bank of the Mississippi near the mouth of the Ohio River. Morgan named the town New Madrid, hoping to please the Spanish, and laid out a town plan that included sites for parks, churches, and schools. He proposed that the schools be supported jointly by families and by the government and wanted the authority to appoint teachers for each of the six English-language schools he planned for the settlement.

Morgan's ambitious colonization plan met with opposition from former general James Wilkinson, an agent of the Spanish, who influenced the officials in New Orleans to reject major parts of it. Morgan abandoned his vision of an American settlement in Spanish territory and never returned to New Madrid, but some of the families he had recruited settled in the area. In 1796, a local priest asked the government to support a school, but nothing came of the request. New Madrid remained primarily a settlement of traders, hunters, boatmen, and soldiers until the Louisiana Purchase. "The earliest-known English language school in the territory opened in about 1799 at the Ramsay settlement near Cape Girardeau," according to William E. Foley in *The Genesis of Missouri*. The school, Mount Tabor, enrolled its few students from the growing number of Americans moving into the district from Kentucky. Foley noted, "By the end of the Spanish period . . . Cape Girardeau [was] the most Americanized of the Spanish administrative districts."

After Americans began settling in New Madrid and other districts west of the Mississippi River in the 1790s, the Spanish opened Upper Louisiana further by allowing a few agricultural land grants to Americans. In 1797, Daniel Morgan Boone, the son of explorer Daniel Boone, discovered the area west of St. Louis on a hunting trip. Daniel Boone and others of his family expressed interest in settling there. The Spanish lieutenant governor in St. Louis awarded a land grant of about a thousand acres near where Femme Osage Creek enters the Missouri River to the Boone family and offered additional land to others the Boones might bring. In 1799, Daniel Boone led his large extended family and many friends to join Daniel Morgan. By that time, as Finiels noted, American immigration to the west side of the Mississippi was in full swing. A census taken in 1800 showed that the area that was to become Missouri had 6,028 inhabitants, and by 1803 the population had increased to about ten thousand. Most of the new settlers were Americans.

American parents settling west of the Mississippi River wanted the best for their children. They did not want them to "grow up barbarous in the wilderness," but in their struggle to provide food and shelter they often could not devote the resources necessary for schooling. Gradually, in settled areas, opportunities for schooling became available as decisions made in Europe dramatically affected the future of the Mississippi valley. Spain returned control of the Louisiana Territory to France in 1800, and in 1803 representatives of President Thomas Jefferson doubled the area of the United States by purchasing the land between the Mississippi River and the Rocky Mountains from Emperor Napoleon of France. The American flag was raised in a ceremony in St. Louis on March 9, 1804. By this time the population of Upper Louisiana had grown to 10,320.

During the time directly before and after the Louisiana Purchase, a few schools opened. Benjamin Johnson taught at a school on Sandy Creek in what is now Jefferson County. Christopher Schewe proposed opening a French and English grammar school in St. Louis, "but he did not meet with encouragement," according to Walter Williams. In 1809, he established a boys' school instead, where he taught English, French, German, geography, and mathematics. Isaac Septlivres advertised that he would teach drawing, geography, and mathematics. Isaac and George Tompkins started a school to teach French and English, but it closed in two years. Most teachers opened schools to earn a living, but many parents could not afford to pay for their children to learn even the most fundamental skills of reading and writing.

Williams wrote that, in 1805, at the first convention called by territorial governor James A. Wilkinson, leaders expressed a desire to set apart some land to maintain "a French and English school in each county, and for the building of a seminary of learning, where not only the French and the English languages, but likewise the dead languages, mathematics, mechanics, natural and moral philosophy and the principles of the constitution of the United States should be taught." The desire to educate all of Missouri's citizens began to take hold early. Achieving statewide educational opportunities would take many decades, but concerned citizens persisted.

In December 1807, leaders called an organizational meeting that marked the beginning of the Ste. Genevieve Academy. The territorial legislature authorized a board of trustees to collect donations and endow the private academy. The group formed a charter establishing the first legally organized school in what was soon to become the Missouri Territory, providing that "the poor and Indian children be taught free." This effort was the beginning of public education in Missouri. A subscription drive raised $3,000. The academy opened in the spring of 1810. Both French and English were taught, but the academy was forced to close when it failed to obtain a land grant from the U.S. government.

Chapter Two

The Missouri Territory

Religion, morality and knowledge being necessary to good government and the happiness of mankind, schools and the means of education shall be encouraged and provided for from the public lands of the United States in said territory, in such manner as Congress may deem expedient.
— Territorial leaders in an act of 1812

As Upper Louisiana became the Missouri Territory, territorial leaders officially recognized the importance of providing a *free* school system. Although the plan was progressive in theory, putting it into practice at that time was not easy. With a small population spread out over thousands of acres, a lack of resources, few books, and even fewer teachers, providing education in the territory would prove difficult, if not impossible.

Three important influences on education came together as families from eastern and southern states settled throughout the territory. Emigrants from New England were accustomed to a "township" plan of government, which provided for small, self-governing schools free of central state control. Those coming from southern states, where wealth was in the hands of a few and large plantations led to a scattered population, favored a system of private schools supported by a few individuals who were able to pay for them. In Missouri, these schools were usually called academies and located in the most populated villages.

The most widely accepted educational influence was Thomas Jefferson's plan, promoting education for all citizens by the state. Jefferson, president when the United States bought the Louisiana Territory from France in 1803, believed that government should educate all of its citizens. In a truly democratic society, he declared, people should be educated to govern themselves. To achieve independence, they needed both a working knowledge of mathematics and the ability to read and express their ideas through writing. Many families agreed with this philosophy, favoring a free public school system, but in the early days private enterprise still dominated educational efforts.

In the early years of territorial settlement and for some time afterward, families often depended on itinerant teachers for what little formal schooling their children received. "Daniel Boone in Missouri," published in the *Missouri Historical Review* in 1909–1910, reports that after 1816 the Boone settlement "employed for a brief season each winter, some traveling schoolmaster, who usually applied to himself the distinguishing title of 'professor.' . . . To this 'academy' the youth of the community came, to study a little and play a great deal more, while the professor amused himself by reading a book." Most would-be schoolmasters did not have much education themselves. In *Stories of Missouri*, John R. Musick told of one prospective teacher who was examined by a committee of trustees from the community. "The applicant was asked if the earth was round or flat. He answered that he wasn't quite sure, but that he was prepared to teach it either way. After a conference on the part of the trustees, it was decided that he should teach that it was flat."

As American settlers moved farther west, the exhausting physical labor necessary to clear fields and build cabins made the fact that the territorial government advocated education for all of little practical importance. On isolated farms or in small communities, there was no time or energy left to think of "schoolin'" the children. In addition, many pioneers thought of education as the responsibility of the parents, a private matter. Some educational opportunities did develop through missions and church enterprises, but territorial schools were rare.

NOTICE IS HEREBY GIVEN,
That Mr. S. Giddings, having procured a convenient house, will give every attention to the instruction of youths, which may be placed under his care. He will intruct in all the branches of science taught in any of the colleges of the United States. The prices of tuition, will be for the quarter commencing June the fourth, four dollars, for those who are only learning to spell ; five dollars for reading and writing, and six dollars for all the higher branches of education.
SALMON GIDDINGS.
St. Louis, May 29th, 1817.   1t-52

Some enterprising newcomers to St. Louis advertised schools promising educational opportunities equal to those in the east. (State Historical Society of Missouri, Columbia)

John Savage opened a school in 1813 near the present-day town of Boonville but closed it after one month because of "Indian troubles." The Reverend Timothy Flint, a New England writer, teacher, Congregational minister, and circuit rider, taught in Cape Girardeau, Florissant, and St. Charles, where he founded a church and school. The school failed. The population in villages was constantly changing, as restless settlers moved on to better opportunities. Teachers sometimes stayed only a few days or one term before moving on themselves.

Wealthy families had little interest in supporting territorial schools. They often employed male tutors or sometimes a governess, an educated woman to care for and supervise their children.

Tutors taught Latin, geography, surveying, calculus, philosophy, fencing, and penmanship. A governess taught table manners and social courtesies so the children could grow up to be the "proper" gentlemen and ladies their parents expected. She might teach harpsichord or oil painting or the dance steps to the waltz. The tutor or governess lived with the family, receiving a small salary plus board and room. Walter Williams in *Missouri, Mother of the West* reports that Eli E. Bass, who owned a large estate near Columbia in Boone County, provided education for his children and those of his neighbors. "He used his riches and influence to good purpose. Among the many benevolent acts of Mr. Bass may be mentioned the fact that he sent to the east for five tutors for his growing family, but he generously invited the children of his neighbors to take lessons also at the same time."

Missions and churches established in villages and towns offered the fundamentals of education through religious teachings. Protestant churches established Sunday schools, sometimes called Sabbath schools, which also taught reading and writing for free, hoping to instill the church's beliefs and values in those attending. Schools established by the Catholic churches taught catechism, reading, and writing. Other denominations started classes on "religion and morality" in settled areas, but most of these suffered the same fate as Reverend Flint's school, not drawing enough students to survive.

Traveling in Missouri and Arkansas in 1818–1819, Henry Schoolcraft, who explored the Ozarks in the early nineteenth century, observed in his journal:

> Schools are also unknown, and no species of learning cultivated. Children are wholly ignorant of the knowledge of books, and have not learned even the rudiments of their own tongue. Thus situated, without moral restraint, bought up in the uncontrolled indulgence of every passion and without a regard of religion, the state of society among the rising generation in this region is truly deplorable. In their childish disputes, boys frequently stab each other with knives, two incidences of which have occurred since our

residence here. No correction was administered in either
case, the act being rather looked upon as a promising trait of
character. They begin to assert their independence as soon as
they can walk, and by the time they reach the age of fourteen,
have completely learned the use of the rifle, the arts of trap-
ping beaver and otter, killing the bear, deer, and buffalo, and
dressing skins and making mockasons and leather clothes.

Missionary circuit riders sometimes brought learning as well
as the gospel to isolated areas. Stopping at cabins and farmhouses
in rural areas for a meal or a place to sleep overnight, they performed marriages and held services. If they had skills in reading,
writing, or "numbers," they sometimes stayed longer to teach
family members willing to learn.

Lillian Nothdurft in *Folklore and Early Customs of Southeast
Missouri* describes the circuit rider:

> The circuit rider, or preacher, as he was called, traveled
> over his territory for the purpose of expounding the Bible
> to people who longed for the comforting messages he
> brought them. He usually owned a few acres of land on
> which he established a home. He spent but little time
> there, however, because he was usually out covering his cir-
> cuit. With his Bible and a few necessities stuffed into his
> saddlebags, he rode his faithful horse for many miles brav-
> ing the dangers of unbeaten trails, inclement weather con-
> ditions, and the opposition of native rowdies who insisted
> that they "was a runnin' things and didn't want no
> preachin' in thish 'ere neck o' the woods."

Once the rider arrived at a cabin, he and the family members
"sang and prayed together and he preached, often arousing their
emotions to the point of shouting, whereby they expressed their
deeply felt religious experience." A forerunner of these riders
was Reverend Jesse Walker, who came from Tennessee to southeast Missouri in 1804 to spread the gospel.

Subscription schools, supported by parents, were popular in
some areas. Some parents paid in farm products, such as potatoes

or beans or chickens, fresh pork, or ham. According to *Ray County Reflections*, "The first school was taught by Meadders Vanderpool in a rude unsightly hut on Ogg's Branch in the summer of 1819. It was a subscription school and the master was paid in calves, buck-skins, and wild honey." The subscribers furnished books and slates and kept the schoolhouse in good repair. The schoolmaster or schoolmistress boarded with parents, sometimes moving every week to another cabin.

One of the earliest types of school in the territory was the "dame school." The dame was an educated woman who taught neighboring children daily in her home for a fee. She prepared boys for grammar school by teaching the alphabet, the catechism, and the Lord's Prayer. She sometimes gave girls the only "formal" education they had. Many thought it was not important or essential to educate girls to perform skills beyond those needed in their home. This attitude prevailed throughout most of the 1800s.

Jean Everling of Holt, Missouri, described the establishment of an early dame school in Clay County:

> The more informed women in the community would pool their resources. Often a widowed lady was the teacher. She gathered as many books as were available at the time, such as *Pilgrim's Progress* and the Bible. Children within walking distance came to her on a daily basis. She taught out of her home. Their contact with the outside world then was religion-based. It was the glue that held the community together. If a traveling minister was around for a week or two, he would be a guest teacher.

The dame school she describes was in Clay County and named Mount Gilead—for the "promised land." The original log cabin was eventually replaced by a two-story frame building.

The dame with few books available might teach numbers by asking the children how many fingers they had on each hand, then how many fingers they had on both hands. She might teach addition by asking, "If you have two nuts in one hand and one in the other, how many have you in both hands?" Records show that dame schools actively educated children in rural counties as late as 1875.

Those who took up teaching advanced many educational theories. One popular approach used the principles of Johann Pestalozzi, a Swiss educational reformer. He based his theory of education on the importance of teaching through the five senses in their natural order of development, using concrete objects. If teaching about an apple, the teacher displayed the apple, cut into it, and examined the seeds. Pestalozzi also introduced field trips as a way to develop sensory insight. A Swiss by the name of Joseph Hertick came to Ste. Genevieve in 1815 to found an academy in a rambling old house ten miles southwest of town. He called his academy The Asylum. Hertick's approach to learning on the Pestalozzi theory provided an education for three future U.S. senators: John R. Jones, Lewis V. Bogy, and Augustus Dodge.

Another popular approach to teaching was developed by Joseph Lancaster, an English educator. His system was to have students teach other students with less knowledge on a subject. Older students taught younger students. Rural schools especially, where all ages and abilities were taught in one room by one teacher, relied on this theory. Lancaster's theory and Pestalozzi's technique are still being used in classrooms today.

However, according to Reverend Timothy Flint, teachers often exaggerated their qualifications. Flint, who stood firm in his commitment to educate those willing to learn, described schools in the ever growing population of St. Louis in a *Missouri Gazette* article:

> I have been amused in reading puffing advertisements in the newspapers. A little subscription school, in which half of the pupils are abecedarians, is a college. One is a Lancastrian school, or a school of "instruction mutuelle." There is the Pestalozzi establishment, with its appropriate emblazoning. There is the agricultural school, the missionary school, the grammar box, the new way to make a wit of a dunce in six lessons and all the mechanical ways of inoculating children

with learning that they may not endure the pain of getting it in the old and natural way.

Little progress was made in educating white children in the Missouri Territory, and even fewer opportunities were available for black children. The long, hard workdays, often from dawn to dusk even for children, left no time for learning. The only free time was on Sunday and sometimes on holidays. During the Colonial period, the *Code Noir*, established by Louis V of France in 1724, was in effect. It provided that slaves were to be instructed in the "Roman, Catholic, and Apostolic faith and baptized" and were to be allowed to observe Sundays and days of obligation. One article in the code held that "slaves who have been named by their masters as tutors for their children" were to be considered as freemen, indicating that some early black residents of the Louisiana Territory must have had educational opportunities. But slaves belonging to different masters were forbidden to gather for any reason.

The Black Codes established by the American territorial government in 1804 were even more restrictive than the *Code Noir*. The fact that slaves could not leave the owner's property without permission or could not assemble restricted opportunities to learn, and it was rare for an owner to allow his slaves any formal schooling. Nevertheless, after the Louisiana Purchase, Catholic owners still saw that their slaves were instructed in their faith. As Protestant missionaries came west to minister to the pioneers and to establish churches, many slave owners allowed or, in some cases, required their slaves to attend Sunday services. The hymns they learned to sing made the long workdays pass a little more quickly, and sometimes they used songs to share feelings or pass messages to fellow slaves.

Some free blacks living in Missouri Territory worked as artists, blacksmiths, and cabinetmakers. John Berry Meachum, who was to contribute significantly to the education of blacks in Missouri, moved in 1815 to St. Louis, where he worked as a carpenter, a cabinetmaker, and a cooper, making barrels. About 1817, John Mason Peck and James Welsh arrived in St. Louis

Born into slavery in Virginia, Meachum learned cabinetmaking and earned enough money to buy his freedom and that of his father. Moving to Kentucky, he married a slave and bought his wife's freedom before moving to St. Louis in 1815. He became a leader in providing education for black children before the Civil War. (Western Historical Manuscript Collection, University of Missouri–St. Louis)

and established the Western Baptist Mission. Peck began a Sabbath school for "Africans," but it caused such resentment among slave owners that he had to require a certificate from the owner for slaves who wanted to attend the school. David and Alberta Shipley wrote about the work of Meachum and Peck in *History of Black Baptists in Missouri:*

> Meachum and his wife became devoted workers with John Mason Peck and John Welch, white Baptist Missionaries, who were beginning their first major assignment among free blacks. A Sunday school was started in the village of St. Louis and within five weeks it had grown from fourteen (14) to ninety (90) pupils. They were taught to read, understand scripture and were involved in services of worship. The attendance was greater than one small room could accommodate, so the group was divided along racial lines. Blacks were organized into a group in 1825 under the leadership of John Berry Meachum, with Peck maintaining somewhat of a supervisory role.

Peck continued to teach black adults and children who came to his Sabbath school in St. Louis, as did some other ministers.

As farms and plantations became more established, sometimes an owner's child or a caring mistress on a plantation might teach slave children or see that they went to school. Jean Henderson of Vienna, Missouri, found accounts of slaves learning to read in the Carver-Danner family history written by Rose Carver Danner:

> Grandmother Myra had little to do in the home, since there were slaves to do the work. She sewed for all of them, however, and the little Negro children grew up wearing the same sort of garment my father and his brother wore for every day—a long shirt-type garment. I don't know what type clothes they had for special occasions, but the long, shirt-type is what they wore at home. The young black children also attended the primitive school the Anderson boys attended, until they were old enough to be put to work, or sold, as the case might be.

Someone teaching slaves a trade would sometimes, out of necessity, teach printed words. If a slave knew how to read and write, other slaves came to him or her to read newspapers and letters or write letters to family members sold away, and slaves who learned to read taught others. But for the most part what slaves learned they taught themselves or learned from one another.

After the Louisiana Purchase, the United States tried to develop plans to turn Native Americans away from their customary nomadic ways. Indian tribes had for centuries educated their children in their own cultural traditions, teaching them the skills they needed to survive as they moved from their villages to hunting grounds and back to their villages each year. Most rejected the white man's ways. Big Soldier, a leader of the Little Osage, voiced the sentiments of his tribe when he said, "Talk to my sons; perhaps they may be persuaded to adopt your fashions . . . for myself, I was born free was raised free and wish to die free."

The U.S. government established posts, or "factories," where Native Americans could "trade without the influence of profiteering, illicit arms traffic and strong drink," to encourage Native Americans to learn agricultural skills. As the U.S.

Indian agent for tribes west of the Mississippi River, William Clark built Fort Osage, a part of this factory system, in 1808 on the right bank of the Missouri River about twenty miles downstream from its junction with the Kansas River.

In the spring of 1816, Mary Easton Sibley came as a bride to Fort Osage with her husband, George C. Sibley, the factor at the trading post. She brought her books and piano, and while living at the fort she taught English to the Indian children in her home, Fountain Green. The fort closed in 1822, and a few years later, the Sibleys moved to St. Charles, where Mary Sibley started Lindenwood College with the help of her husband.

Like many French missionaries to the Louisiana Territory, Rose Philippine Duchesne of the Order of the Sacred Heart of Jesus longed to serve Indians in the New World. She arrived in New Orleans in late May 1818, ill from the long voyage, and traveled up the Mississippi to St. Louis, expecting to teach Indian children. Bishop Louis William DuBourg almost sent her back to France because of her health but instead sent her to St. Charles to establish a boarding school for wealthy French and English girls. She also managed to open a free day school for girls, the first free school for girls west of the Mississippi.

In *Hardship and Hope*, Carla Waal and Barbara Korner published excerpts from Duchesne's letters about her work in Missouri. On October 18, 1818, she wrote from St. Charles, "the remotest village in the United States. It is situated on the Missouri, which is frequented only by those trading with the Indians who live not very far away from here, but I have not seen any little Indian girls since we came here." She added that Bishop DuBourg had appointed one day a week when the sisters could teach black children.

On December 28, 1823, Duchesne wrote from Florissant, where the sisters now had a convent, and a few months later she was much encouraged that the Jesuits had started a seminary for Indian boys nearby. She hoped that the sisters could take up work with the girls, writing, "Food will cost very little; we have a place to house them; and we shall beg clothing for them." By March 1825 she had two girls for her Female Seminary Academy

Sister Rose Philippine Duchesne came to St. Louis from her native France in 1818, at age forty-eight, to work as a missionary to the Indians for the Order of the Sacred Heart of Jesus. Sent to St. Charles, she started the first free school for girls west of the Mississippi. By the time of her death in 1852, she had established schools and seminaries for white, black, and Indian children in Missouri, Kansas, and Louisiana. She was canonized on July 3, 1988. (State Historical Society of Missouri, Columbia)

and by June six were enrolled, but in the summer of 1826 the seminary had to be closed.

As Duchesne frequently mentioned in her letters, the U.S. government and immigrants from the settled states were pushing the Indian tribes farther west. It was not until the 1840s, after living in St. Charles, Florissant, and St. Louis, teaching

HARMONY MISSION FOR THE OSAGES-1821-BATES COUNTY

At the request of the Osage, the United Foreign Missionary Society of New York sent missionaries to open a school in western Missouri in 1821. Located in what is today Bates County, Harmony Mission offered classes to Osage, Delaware, Omaha, and Cherokee children. (Mural in the Missouri State Capitol by William Knox, photograph by Wright Studios; State Historical Society of Missouri, Columbia)

and caring for orphans, that she finally realized her dream of working among the Indians. From Sugar Creek, Kansas, the village of the Potawatomi, she wrote happily of her work there. The children she taught gave her the name Woman Who Prays Always. She never learned their language, but she was loved and understood by the Native Americans she finally had the opportunity to work among.

Missionaries from the Presbyterian and Dutch Reformed churches established Harmony Mission, the first school in Bates County, organized in 1821 for the education of Osage and other Native American children. The United Foreign Missionary Society of New York City sent a group of ten adult males, fifteen adult females, and ten children to the isolated location. Reverend N. B. Dodge was to be the superintendent, and Amasa Jones and Miss Ettress were to teach. The missionaries had limited success. According to a report,

To clothe, board and teach them the English language and then to teach the common branches of education and also to teach them how to work was a work of such herculean proportions that nothing short of the greatest patience and perserverence [sic] and the feeling that they were working for a greater than earthly reward could ever have induced people to carry it on. . . . The pupils were Osage, Delaware, Omaha, and Cherokee Indians. . . . most were bright and as capable of learning as white children.

After Missouri gained statehood in 1821, efforts to remove Native Americans westward intensified, and in a treaty signed in 1825 the Osage gave up all their land in Missouri. No federal reservations were established in Missouri. Only churches and missionaries continued offering education to the few remaining Native Americans, meeting with limited success in "civilizing" them and instilling in them their own religious beliefs.

Although "the means of education" had shown little progress by 1821, historian Duane Meyer notes in *Heritage of Missouri*, "One of the most significant cultural advances during the territorial period was the establishment of schools throughout the area."

Chapter Three

A New State

While the people as a rule were not educated, many of them very illiterate as far as education was concerned, they were thoroughly self-sustaining when it came to the knowledge required to do things that brought about a plentiful supply of the necessities of life.

— Alexander Majors, *Seventy Years on the Frontier*

During the early 1800s, more Americans eagerly pressed westward each year, looking for a place to establish homes and put down roots. By 1820 the white population of the Missouri Territory had grown to almost sixty thousand, with the slave population at more than ten thousand, as pioneers eager for land continued to pour into the territory. Money was scarce, but land was plentiful. Public lands were for sale to the highest bidder, with the minimum set at two dollars an acre.

An Osage elder remembered that settlers "came like ants," and Reverend John Mason Peck wrote, "The newcomers, like a mountain torrent, poured into the country faster than it was possible to provide corn for bread-stuffs." They came pushing or pulling handcarts filled with tools and seeds and a few belongings. Some carried chickens. Some held ropes leading livestock, possibly a few goats or a milk cow. The luckiest ones had a small plow, but most owned just a hoe, a scythe, and an ax. Wagon

Flatboats, along with canoes and rafts, provided transportation on Missouri's rivers for pioneer families arriving from eastern states. The flat bottoms allowed the boats to float in shallow water, and the board sides with square corners kept people and provisions from falling overboard. (State Historical Society of Missouri, Columbia)

after wagon came through St. Louis, each pulled by a team of horses or oxen, carrying a husband with his new bride or families with as many as eleven or twelve barefoot children.

Those families who owned books often had to leave them behind in order to bring necessities. If there was room for only one book, it was most often the family Bible that was brought to the wilderness. Learning to read from the Bible was the first and only experience many pioneer children had with written words. Yet some families did make room for additional books. In *Pioneer Schools of Monroe County*, Zelma Menefee recounts,

No settlement had been made within the boundaries of Monroe County until 1820 when Ezra Fox and friends came

Most families emigrating west did not have room for books, but for some new-comers books were important enough to bring. Often, however, building a log cabin for shelter and clearing the fields for crops had to take priority over learning. (State Historical Society of Missouri, Columbia)

from Kentucky. . . . The earliest pioneers were too busy carving out the wilderness to devote much time to reading or thinking of education, yet many of them came from cultured homes in Virginia and Kentucky. The covered wagons which carried them to this area also carried the Bible and often books such as "Life of Washington," "History of the Revolutionary War," and the works of Shakespeare and Scott, as well as the classics, Dickens and Thackeray and others.

Most pioneers in Missouri were English-speaking Old Stock Americans from Ohio, Virginia, Kentucky, North Carolina, and Tennessee. They settled where the soil was rich and tillable, on land with access to water. Missouri had thick forests providing wood for buildings and fences, and wild game was plentiful. But life on the frontier and its daily hardships took a toll on the children. Some died at birth. Often parents would not name their newborns until several months after their births, fearing they would not survive. Older children died from accidents, disease, or in some cases starvation. All the children in a family could fall ill with cholera, from contaminated food, or with typhoid fever and die within days or weeks of one another. Many, however, seemed to thrive. Reverend Timothy Flint's impressions of the numerous children passing through St. Charles are included in A *History of the Pioneer Families of Missouri:*

> But they were hearty and hungry, and their bread and milk was as rich a feast to them as a king's supper. There was no lack of children then. Every family had ten or a dozen of them, and some had as many as twenty, all healthy, hearty, active little fellows . . . it cost nothing to support them, as they usually made their own way; so each little new-comer received a hearty welcome, and was sent on his way rejoicing.

Missouri gained statehood in 1821 with no restriction on slavery, and some early settlers lived on large farms or plantations with their slaves; but most newcomers lived in log cabins, miles from the nearest neighbor. Unlike the French, who settled in villages, the new emigrants from the east had no neighbors to turn to, and children often had no contact with anyone outside their own family, having only brothers and sisters for company. A trip to town or to visit a relative could take days of travel. Surviving on the frontier was a constant challenge. Even those parents who could read or write themselves found little time to teach their children the alphabet, reading, writing, or numbers. The experiences of Nancy Caroline Moser of Crocker in Pulaski County, told in *Pioneers of the Ozarks* by Lennis Broadfoot, must have reflected that of the children of many pioneers.

> I have always lived in the hills of Pulaski County and don't know nothin' about other places, and I never traveled none, 'cause I have always had my nose held right down to the grindin' stone to make a livin' for the family.
>
> I never got to go to school none, and all the larnin' I got was jist what my mother larned me. We had an old blue-black spellin' book an' she would set down late at night after we got through with our work sich as cardin' wool, spinnin', knittin', weavin' carpets, and hullin' beans, and call me up to her, and give me lessons out of this old spellin' book, by the light of the old tallow candlestick.
>
> She kept this up till she larned me jist enough to know how to read a little, and as soon as we was able, we bought us a coal oil lamp, and I thought they was the finest thing and give the brightest light of anything I ever see'd. So I kept on studyin' and larnin' till I got so I could read the Bible, and that's about all I've read in my life, and nothin' gives me so much contentment and pleasure as to set down by the light of my old coal oil lamp after my day's work is done, and read my Bible.

As emigration from Central Europe increased, settlers separated by miles of rough rocky trails were also separated by the differing languages they spoke and by differing customs and religious beliefs. Neighbors with their "strange and different ways" sometimes had nothing in common. Emigrant families settling in villages with similar beliefs and the same language were able to place greater emphasis on educating their children. They worked together, socialized with each other, and provided a rudimentary education for their "young uns," teaching from whatever books were available.

Wealthy southern landowners in Missouri influenced the opening of private academies and seminaries. Female seminaries were private boarding schools for young ladies, supported by tuition fees. Girls could choose from a number of classes, including music, English grammar and composition, history, astronomy, natural and moral philosophy, and geography, and they could learn skills such as embroidery, cut paperwork, and filigree (jewelry and fine needlework). Strict attention was devoted to mental, moral, and social instruction. A typical newspaper advertisement promised "to instruct young ladies in all the solid and mental branches of a finished education." Mrs. Francis Carr established her seminary in St. Louis in 1820 with a student enrollment "limited to twenty," with each session lasting five months. Mary Bingham opened a school for girls in Franklin in Howard County. After the death of her husband in 1823 she moved to a farm in Saline County, where a plantation culture was developing, and opened a new school there, admitting boys as well as girls. Her son, the great Missouri artist George Caleb Bingham, studied art and served as a janitor for the school as a teenager. In 1820 J. B. C. Washington operated a select coeducational school in Franklin to instruct young ladies and gentlemen "in most of the solid and ornamental branches of a polite English education."

The General Assembly chartered (approved) some academies after Missouri attained statehood. They were managed by trustees elected annually. Unchartered schools were founded by an individual or organization under the general laws for partnership and operated privately through fees and donations without support from the state. Academies most closely resembled the public schools of today because of their "branches" offering basic education in reading, writing, and arithmetic.

The classes at these academies typically included Latin, Greek, mathematics, drawing, reading and writing, literature, and orthography (spelling). Students received instruction in basic ethics (morals) and aesthetics (culture appreciation). The cost of classes was set by the owner, who was often the only teacher, and the fee covered expenses plus a profit. The first class taken might cost five dollars per quarter, with each additional class costing four dollars. In 1839 Friedrich Steines, a German immigrant, opened Oakfield Academy in Franklin County where sons of many St. Louis German immigrants received a classical education. By 1850, there were approximately two hundred academies in Missouri for boys who had completed studies in a country school.

Officials in the new state of Missouri, however, continued to be concerned about establishing a statewide public school system. The first Missouri constitution had declared that "one school, or more, shall be established in each township as soon as practicable and necessary, where the poor shall be taught gratis [free]." A free common public school system was the hope of some parents, but others, proud and self-reliant, were offended by the words *poor* and *gratis*. To these families, sending their children to a public school was the same as accepting charity, acknowledging that they were too poor to educate their own children. Some in Missouri called these "pauper schools," meaning schools for the very poor.

Although several laws had been passed relating to education earlier, the first serious effort to establish statewide policies in support of schools came in 1835. The General Assembly created a "board of commissioners for literary purposes," considered to be the first state board of education. The law provided that schools should be in session for at least six months each year and that residents of a county, by a two-thirds majority vote, could tax themselves to support schools.

The distance separating farm families and small villages from one another presented the major problem as Missouri tried to develop free public schools. Even in more settled areas, the General Assembly found most school townships in complete disorder as far as their obligation to manage the public land intended for schools. Some townships had scattered records. Some had no records of transactions made. Some had no money in their school fund and had made no effort to build a school.

Henry S. Geyer is considered "the father" of Missouri's public school system. Born of German parents in Maryland in 1790, Geyer studied law with an uncle in Virginia, served in the U.S. Army as a captain in the War of 1812, and moved to St. Louis to practice in 1815. He served in the state legislature during the 1820s and 1830s and wrote the School Act of 1839, basing it on the Jeffersonian philosophy of education. The act was considered significant because it created permanent funds to support schools and outlined a system of education, including a state university. It made possible the organization of townships, to be governed by township councils, for the purpose of creating school districts. However, because the act was complicated, difficult to understand, and provided only small sums of money, it was never put into effect. Numerous enactments followed until the act of 1853, when the school laws were revised, continuing to incorporate Geyer's ideas.

Included in later school enactments were specific rules for commissioners and inspectors. Two or more were to visit and examine all instructors every three months and were to replace instructors unable to pass the examination. The inspectors could also demand exercises from the pupils, referred to as "scholars," to evaluate their proficiency in learning. A board of trustees was to decide on the number of children to receive an education free of charge and determine each teacher's fee. An act of January 17, 1825, had specified, "Scholars should be taught reading, writing, arithmetic and the English Grammar." As more Americans arrived from eastern states to settle the new lands opening in Missouri, English had become the most widely spoken language in the state, and English was required in newly formed public schools and generally accepted as the common language.

However, the French language still prevailed in schools into the 1830s and 1840s in some areas, including St. Louis and Ste. Genevieve. In "Recollections of Early St. Louis," Jesse Benton Frémont tells of a French primary school she attended in St. Louis whose teacher, a "quiet, gentle man," was in charge of her class. "Here in Saint Louis we were let to go to school; chiefly for the practice in French among other children."

It makes me smile to look back at that word "school" which had not the first idea of studies, of punctuality, or discipline attached to it as I knew it. The going there each morning was as good as playing truant. . . .

When we did reach the school we were consigned to Madam Savary who did not teach, but who looked after us; a small vivacious Swiss-Frenchwoman with a mania for making preserves and doing fine sewing. Monsieur Savary was capable of far more than was required of him. I think he had put away his pride and resigned himself to what he could, not what he would, do. He . . . always wore a short-waisted very long and full-skirted frock coat of gray, with collar and cuffs of black velvet, a sort of uniform for teachers which you often see in old-fashioned French illustrations. He was quiet, gentle and forbearing, and had need to be so as there were about thirty girls, from six to sixteen—of course not a fraction of a boy in a French school—and not one with any intentions of study or habit of discipline; good-natured enough, but trying. They may have learned something. We were there only for easy handling of familiar French; and except some spelling, and reading aloud in *Telemachus*, I do not recall anything of lessons. . . . By one o'clock Aunt Sara had come for us to go home and as this was our dinner hour we made no delays.

By the 1840s many German immigrants had arrived in Missouri, and they continued to speak their language in villages such as Westphalia and Hermann and in Perry County and St. Louis. Wanting to preserve their language and culture in the New World, some early German immigrants started schools. Nicholas Hesse, who settled in an isolated area of central Missouri in 1835, brought a German-speaking teacher for his six children. The Old Order Lutherans who settled in Perry County established a school in Altenburg in 1839 that later became known as the Log Cabin Seminary, providing education for both young men and young women. German Lutherans, Catholics, and other denominations provided schooling for children of immigrants, and German Methodists established a school in

In the 1830s more and more emigrants from European countries heard about opportunities in Missouri. Some Germans came in groups formed by emigration societies. The largest group to set out for Missouri was from Saxony. Led by a charismatic Lutheran pastor, they arrived in St. Louis in the winter of 1838–1839 and eventually moved to Perry County, where they established a "log cabin college" to educate the young men and women of the group. They survived the first winter with the help of American neighbors and eventually formed the Missouri Synod of the Lutheran Church, which established Concordia Seminary and church schools in several parts of the state. (State Historical Society of Missouri, Columbia)

Warren County. As later immigrants arrived, even the "free-thinkers" sent their children to church schools to learn German.

The town of Hermann, which had been founded in 1837–1838 to be "German in every particular," opened its own school in the late 1840s to preserve German customs, language, and values. As Adolf E. Schroeder reported in *Little Germany on the Missouri*, "On March 10, 1849, the Missouri General Assembly granted a charter to Hermann, sanctioning the use of the German language in instruction in all branches of science and education, and stipulating that the school was to be known as the 'German School of Hermann' and that it 'forever remain a German School.'"

In the mid-1800s, subscription schools and private academies were teaching a variety of subjects in many parts of Missouri. In 1854, Clay County approved a tax to raise $1,000 to build a school on a lot obtained from W. L. Watkins. The octagonal structure allowed better air circulation and more light. Franklin began as a subscription school, but in 1865 it became an academy of "higher learning" until free schooling became available. The building is now preserved at Watkins Mill State Park. (State Historical Society of Missouri, Columbia)

Private subscription schools, popular during territorial days, continued to be formed by neighboring parents agreeing to provide both a school and a teacher. Such groups built a school building or made space available in a shed, barn, or abandoned log cabin and hired a schoolmaster for a term or quarter. The term was two to four months in the winter and two to four months in the spring. The length of the term was determined by what the parents (called subscribers) could afford to pay, by the need for children to work in the fields or mines, and by the availability of a teacher. The schoolmaster or mistress was paid by the term or one to two dollars per month "per scholar." As the state became more involved in education, state support was sometimes available for poor children to attend a subscription school if their parents signed or made their "mark" certifying that they could not afford to pay tuition.

The first high school was established in St. Louis in 1853. Parents wanted a share in the control of education and selected a board directly responsible to "the people" who desired a more advanced education for their children than elementary schools could provide. On opening day, 70 pupils were admitted after a rigid examination. The theory was that only "select" students should be allowed to attend. By the next year, the number of pupils had increased to 110. Courses of study included higher arithmetic, grammatical analysis, composition, higher algebra, plane and spherical geometry, trigonometry, Latin, and German.

In March 1866 the Missouri General Assembly passed a public school bill eliminating the authority of local districts to charge tuition. However, a few communities continued the practice, not wanting their children to attend a "pauper school," which some parents considered a reflection on their ability to educate their children. Others resisted free schools because they did not want the schools overcrowded with poor children or children of immigrant parentage.

Chapter Four

The Rural Schoolhouse

It seemed, as I recall it, a lonely little house of scholarship with its playground worn so bare, that even the months of sun and idleness failed to bring forth any grass. But that humble little school had a dignity of a fixed and far off purpose. . . . It was the outpost of civilization. It was the advance guard of the pioneer, driving the wilderness farther into the west. It was life preparing wistfully for the future.

— James Rooney, *Journeys from Ignorant Ridge*

James Rooney was writing about his school in Texas, but his words ring true for children in Missouri who went to log-cabin schools. For most of the children in Missouri who lived on farms in sparsely populated areas, or in isolated Ozark regions, "schooling" took place in a one-room log building during much of the nineteenth century. The log-cabin schools often originated as subscription schools built by parents, because of their cheap and easy construction and their durability. Some eventually became common public schools under the management and jurisdiction of the state.

Historians have suggested that Swedish settlers arriving in America were responsible for this new home-building technique for the frontier wilderness—*the log cabin*. Dense woodlands of shortleaf pine, black walnut, black oak, eastern cottonwood, bur oak, black cherry, white and scarlet oak, and other trees covered

McKendree Chapel

The first church built by Methodists in Cape Girardeau County dates from 1819. It is of log construction with a shingle roof and plank floors. The chapel was regularly used as a school as well as for religious services and camp revival meetings. (State Historical Society of Missouri, Columbia)

one-third of Missouri, so the materials needed for building log structures were readily available. One-room chinked log cabins provided shelter from strong winds, drenching rainstorms, and freezing winter blizzards. The cabins could withstand arrows and rifle bullets, if necessary.

Some of the earliest log schools were built without using a single iron nail or any metal hardware. Wooden pins were used for nails, hinges, and door latches. The fireplace provided heat and a place to cook food. Sometimes a lean-to, a structure with a roof supported by poles and attached to the side of the cabin, was added to shelter the teacher's horse or a buggy. Most cabins were built close to the ground and supported on stone pillars, usually one on each corner and one in the middle.

Only two tools were necessary to build a cabin: an ax to cut logs to the required size and a froe, used to cut shingles or roof

Most early schools were small with few comforts for the teacher or the scholars. This school, built in 1894, was in the Accident School District in Barry County, southeast of Cassville, and is the last log school built in the county. The photograph dates from 1914. (Gift of F. A. Meador, State Historical Society of Missouri, Columbia)

boards. When the unhewn rough logs were ready for building, neighbors, ropes, and farm animals provided the means to raise them one on top of another. The spaces between logs were chinked with moss, clay, mud, and straw. Hands, rather than trowels, smoothed the clay between the cracks. Each side of the building was anywhere from ten to twelve feet long, and the ceilings were from seven to twelve feet high. In *Annals of Kansas City*, Stephen C. Ragan, an early teacher, describes mixing mortar for log-cabin schools:

> In making the mortar needed for these log houses, straw mixed in the mud was as essential as hair is in our lime mortar. Mud mortar was made by digging up a quantity of dirt, pouring water over it, covering it with straw, and then throwing a quantity of shelled corn on the straw that had been added to the mud and water. Then the swine were

called up. When they smelled the corn, they went for it, rooting and tramping, thus producing a well-mixed mortar with which to daub the cracks between the logs.

Windows and doors were formed when a space the length of the logs was left during building. The openings for windows were covered with animal skins, gunnysacks, a blanket, greased paper, or sometimes a plank attached below the window with leather straps so it could be opened and closed. "Stick-and-dirt" chimneys were commonly made from sticks, short logs, straw, and mud. The sticks were daubed with clay or mud. Every stick needed to be completely covered so the cabin did not catch fire. The back walls of the fireplace were surrounded by loosely piled rocks. Some fireplaces were so large they could hold a log five to six feet long. Log schoolhouses built without fireplaces were not used during winter months.

Floors were typically left as dirt, or dirt covered with straw. The straw made the floor warmer for bare feet, but it was a breeding place for fleas. Bites from fleas and other insects caused constant scratching and wiggling among scholars. In some cases, a puncheon floor or a plank floor was laid down. A puncheon floor consisted of logs split so that one side was flat and smooth, while the other remained rounded and covered with tree bark. Plank floors tended to buckle and stub toes. Both kinds of wood floors caused slivers in bare feet. In winter, stones were heated in the fire and placed under the students' feet on the dirt or wooden floor to help keep them warm.

A shared writing shelf was the only desk in the earliest log schools. An opening the size of several logs was left as the building was constructed, creating an oblong window extending from the door to the corner of the building. Holes were bored into the wall directly under this window. Pegs or pins hammered into the holes held up a long piece of smooth lumber or a puncheon log shelf. This board was used as a desk or held books and dinner pails.

Benches were made of puncheon logs. With an auger, two holes were bored into each end of the rounded, rough side of the

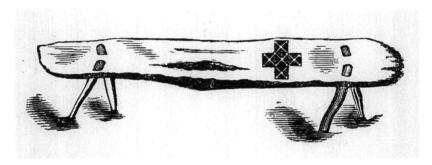

An ax, a saw, and sharp iron wedges were the only tools necessary to cut down a tree and split the trunk. To make a puncheon seat, the pieces were sawed to the length needed, holes were cut out on the rough side of the log, and the legs of the seat were fitted to the holes and attached. (State Historical Society of Missouri, Columbia)

log. Then, pegs or legs were driven into the holes. Anywhere from three to eight students sat on the puncheon bench, depending on the length of the log. Students sat facing the teacher. The teacher sat on a log bench facing the students. The benches for the children were not adjustable. They were usually the best height for taller students, but tiresome for the younger boys and girls with short legs that did not reach the floor. Children sat all day with their feet dangling. Often their legs went to sleep. Those sitting on the ends had to brace themselves to try to keep from falling off when someone leaned toward them or took up too much space. In some cases, a child fell asleep and toppled off the bench. Naomi Baker Alley, who attended Lamine School on the border of Cooper and Pettis counties, says that her grandmother, Susan Adams Ball, often told of accompanying her older sister to school before she was of school age. "In the afternoon she went to sleep and toppled off the old puncheon seat and exposed herself (an expression used in those days). She was so embarrassed that she ran out of the schoolhouse and hid in the brush until school was out."

Kerosene or "coal oil" lamps lit the school on dark cloudy days. The base of the lamp was filled with kerosene. A knob on the side of the base raised a wick made from cotton that soaked up the kerosene. After the wick was lit, a round glass chimney (open on the top) was placed over the base. Some schools had wall brackets to hold the lamps, but the lighting was dim and hard to see by.

After the 1840s, a "boxwood" stove generally sat in the center of the classroom. Coal or firewood provided the heat. The coals were banked at the end of the school day to help start the next day's fire. Because corncobs ignited easily, students often brought gunnysacks filled with corncobs to use in starting the fire. The students sitting closest to the stove roasted their fronts or their backs, depending on which direction they faced. On the coldest days, the heat reached only the children sitting closest to the stove. The ones sitting farther away were always cold. Caring teachers rotated their students every hour or so, bringing those in the back closer to the warmth of the stove.

Box stoves had a flue made of several pipes joined together; this flue extended up to the ceiling then led over to an opening in a chimney, or it went straight up through a hole in the roof. The smoke went up the flue, and so did ashes. If the flue wasn't cleaned out regularly, it became heavy from ashes, and stovepipes sometimes fell apart at the joints, dumping the ashes over students sitting underneath.

"Spit boxes" were occasionally used under the desks of the tobacco chewers. But one student recalled in *Wilson's History of Hickory County*, "A fellow could chew tobacco and squirt the tobacco juice into the fire place to hear it fry, with great ease and satisfaction. Nobody but a numb-skull would have bought a spittoon if he had known of such a thing."

In the barren, dark, damp log schoolhouse, there was sometimes one colorful picture hanging on the wall: George Washington, with a white powdered wig, a stiff collar, and a pleasant expression. In some schools, Washington's picture was joined, after the Civil War, by a picture of President Abraham Lincoln. Fondly called "Uncle Abe," the president was credited with helping the common people and abolishing slavery, and many schools for black children were named for him. And always there was a flag, whether folded neatly or displayed outdoors or hung on pegs indoors. Love of country and patriotism were expressed in a typical handwriting lesson.

> I love the name of Washington.
> I love my country, too.
> I love the flag, the dear old flag.
> The red, the white, the blue.

Students carried water for the school from a creek or spring or the well of a neighbor, often as far as mile down the road. The water bucket was made from wooden slats bound with metal strips or rope. When it rained, the bucket was set outside to catch rainwater. If the creek was frozen, snow was piled high in the bucket and brought inside to melt. Wallace McClellan in Callaway County remembered that "in real hot times early in the season . . . teacher wouldn't let everybody go back and get a sip of water. She'd point to some kid to take the bucket up and down the line, and let everybody have a sip of water out of the dipper." When the children were outdoors they drank water directly from the creek. Few wells were dug for the first schools. That was more than parents could afford, both in the time it took to find water and dig the well and in the expense of providing a pulley and handle to raise and lower the bucket.

Calvin W. Smith Jr., a teacher in Newton County, recalled how his students got drinks at recess and noon:

> At one school where I taught, the school board decided it was inconvenient for the children to have to go down to the spring for a drink, because it was between two small ravines. So, they built a heavy plank floor with wide cracks in it, rested it on top of the ravines, installed a hand pump, and furnished one tin cup. At recess and noon one of the larger boys would man the pump handle, and would keep a steady stream of water going, while the pupils stood around waiting their turn to drink. The favorite pastime was washing their feet under this stream of water. The water dripped back through the cracks into the spring, then it was pumped

up again and the children drank it. Strangest thing of all
was that hardly ever a child missed school because of illness.

The water dipper might be a store-bought tin cup but was
usually homemade from a gourd cut in half. The seeds of the
gourd were scooped out and the outer shell was then dried,
forming a dipper. Everyone drank from the same dipper. Putting
a frog in the water bucket was a favorite prank. When someone
screamed, the hunt for the prankster began.

The water bucket and common dipper led to the spread of
childhood diseases. Sometimes schools had to close for a week
or two when an epidemic of smallpox or measles infected the
students. In the late 1800s, children started to bring their own
cups, and in 1914 the State Department of Education issued a
statement advising school officials that the time had come "in
our state when an open bucket and common drinking cup
should no longer be tolerated."

A schoolhouse was typically built on an acre or more of land,
usually donated because it had soil too poor to raise crops or was
in a densely wooded area that was difficult to clear, on top of a
steep hill, or by a creek that flooded in the spring. The boundary
for a play area was set by a fence (with the possible presence of
a bull on the other side), a road, a cornfield, a creekbed, woods,
six-foot-tall prairie grass, scrub oak, or clumps of buffalo grass.
The most important boundary was based on the distance at
which the children could still hear a "calling out" of the teacher
to "form a line" or could hear the handheld bell ringing. One
teacher at Hawk School, in Iron County, banged on the sides of
the school and yelled, "Come in to books."

Judge Jeremiah Cravens in the *History of Jasper County*
described the first log school he attended: "The jams on each side
and the back were made of rough rock and the balance of the
chimney was made of sticks daubed with red clay. . . . In the side
of the door a nail was driven into the wall and on this was suspended a little forked stick about six inches long, which every
scholar took with him when he went out during the hours of study.
No scholar was allowed to go out till this little fork was returned."

Those parents who could afford the time and cost provided small roofed structures on the school grounds for the convenience of the children. Known by many names—an outhouse, a necessary house, a privy (private), or a toilet—they inspired many pranks and stories. Before toilet paper was available, old catalogs were often used in its place. These buildings were on the grounds of Franklin School in Clay County. (Photo by author)

Sometimes parents provided small outhouses on the school grounds, which afforded privacy when a student needed to "go out" to use a restroom. If there was no outhouse, or "necessary house," students used the woods or bushes for cover, with boys going to one side of the school and girls to the other. Guy Howard, called the "Walking Preacher of the Ozarks," taught and preached in Mulberry School, a log cabin in the northeast corner of Hickory County. "The school board director showed him the school. . . . When Guy asked about restrooms, the director told him, 'The girls go up the north holler and the boys go down the south holler—and if'n you ketch any o' them boys goin' up the north holler, you whup the daylights outa-em." Or boys went over one hill and girls went over another. Usually there was one outhouse, but sometimes a privy (private) was built for the boys and another one for the girls. A traditional sign was sawed in the doors. The sign for the boys' privy was a sun, while a figure of a moon was sawed on the girls' door.

The privy was approximately four square feet. It had one door and no windows. There was a latch on the inside to fasten the door. Usually a "vault," or hole, was dug in the ground, and the outhouse was built around it. Lime was scattered inside the hole to keep flies away. A box was placed over the vault, with one or two openings sawed out of the top board. After an outhouse had been used for a few years and the stench had become unbearable, a new vault was dug, and the outhouse building was moved. Wind sometimes blew these small houses over, and pranksters thought it was fun to push them on their sides. Velma (Burch) Pierce, a teacher in a Texas County rural school, recalled, "I arrived at school early A.M. to find the outdoor (John) toilet had been moved and placed over our water pump for a well house in such a way we couldn't pump water. When the children arrived one said—'Oh, my! No water—and no place to put it.'"

In *Pulaski County Rural Schools*, Claudine Groce describes the outdoor toilet, quoting a former teacher at Sheeley or Oaklawn School in District 10:

> The school ground was never fenced . . . the wooded ground where the building stood was a hog pasture so the hogs could feed on the acorns. It was not at all unusual to come to school and find mama pig building a nest in the toilet to have her babies. But the sad part was when she got all the way in the door shut from the inside and there she stayed. What a mess!

Students went outside during hail or rain and in drifting snow to use the privy. Hornets, wasps, bees, flies, mosquitoes, toads, snakes, and an occasional larger animal such as a raccoon, skunk, or possum took refuge there, and the user had to be cautious about opening the door. In an article in *Gateway Heritage*, Lisa Heffernan quoted a student from Callaway County who worried, "There would be this mud dubbers' nest up in the corner [of the outhouse] and you'd go out there and you'd wonder if there were mud dubbers working on the other side of the bench. You'd always wonder about that, you know."

The majority of schools were named after the person who donated the land, a feature of the terrain, or any wildlife in the area. Typical were school names found in Montgomery County—Pine Knot, Maple Grove, Young, Eckler, Meadow Lark, Price's Branch, Sunbeam, Crab Apple, Honey Locust, Devault, Bell, Bridge, Rhineland, Best Bottom, Whiteside, Mudd, Orange Blossom, Possum Trot, Freedom, and Swope, the latter named after Jacob Swope, who donated two acres of land.

Laclede County schools were named Hog Wallow, Shady Grove, Orchard View, Pleasant Grove, Tyrone, and Stultz. A school near Houston, Missouri, was named Racket Ridge after a fight by boys on that ridge. Two Koshkonong rural schools were named King's Point and Barren Hollow. Still Camp Ditch School, outside Poplar Bluff, took its name from the nearby ditch. A rural school in Callaway County named Boulware got a new name after students read a book entitled *St. Eunice*. They liked the story and name so much that they began calling their school St. Eunice. Eventually, the name was changed on official county records. In Maries County, schoolhouses were named Buzzard Rock in Excelsior and Hay Holler in Victory.

In *Our Storehouse of Missouri Place Names*, Robert L. Ramsay notes that in Franklin County, in 1874, residents called a rural school Reed's Defeat, because the boys had made life so miserable for the teacher, a man named Reed, that "the directors finally had to discharge him." And a school near the Pettis/Cooper county line was named Rawhide. Residents in the vicinity thought the name originated from a nearby tannery.

Roundtop School in Dekalb County was named for the shape of its roof. Cotton Patch School in the Boonslick area got its name because a man had planted several acres of cotton there before the school was built. And Pea Ridge School got its name because the land it was built on was so poor "you could only grow peas on it."

The school called Camp Ground was near a church where camp meetings were held and people "tented on the old Camp

Ground." Another school was named after an incident from the Civil War. Southern bushwhackers were in the area looking for able-bodied men. Mr. Holland hid so well from the southerners that they couldn't find him, earning him the nickname "Wild Cat Holland." When the land was used for a school site, the building was called Wild Cat School after Mr. Holland.

Round Prairie in Newton County was named because it was located on a high, round, treeless knoll. Some Benton County schools were Prairie Flower, Evening Shade, Fraction Point (because it sat on top of a rocky hill), and Mt. Lasca (named for the teacher's favorite poem). Some think Cabbage Neck School in Lafayette County was named after a cave where settlers stored their cabbages. Cold Water School in Wright County was at a source of very cold springwater, and Buzzard Roost in Pulaski County was named for the buzzards that roosted in its rafters while it was under construction. In the Pulaski School District, the story is told that those building one school ran out of building materials and needed more to finish the structure, so they decided to name it Needmore. *History of Lafayette County Missouri Rural Schools* describes how Egypt School District 13 in that county was named: "Egypt Bottoms was given to the general area of the floodplain across the southern end of Ray County by Joseph Roy, a French trapper. . . . In 1845 he was flooded out [and] told some neighbors he was 'going back to Egypt' comparing the fertility of the soil to that of the Nile River delta."

Although the furnishings of their schools were simple, most children were excited about going to school. They made new friends. They had other children of their own age to play with. They could learn to read and write. Many had helped in some way to build the school by mixing mud with straw for chinking or bringing food—biscuits, pickles, sliced ham, and applesauce cake—for neighbors building the school. And they smoothed the dirt floor with rakes and chopped firewood for the fireplace. They sensed their parents' excitement and enthusiasm in planning a school and hiring a teacher. Most rural families lived in log cabins, and though many of the early schools were not the equal of the poorest cabin, the scholars didn't expect any more in a new school building. There was great pride in knowing this was their school. It was a luxury—even a retreat from the hard daily chores and labor of farming or working in a coal mine at coaling time. Some children wanted to learn and went to school eagerly and willingly. Some went only because their parents sent them and it was a way to escape work at home. Whatever the circumstances, the school fulfilled the parents' goal and their aspirations to educate their children.

Some children did not remember the schoolhouse pleasantly in later years. Claude Phillips quotes John W. Henry, the super- intendent of common schools in Missouri in the 1860s, recalling his days as a scholar in a log-cabin school.

> With an inexplicable infatuation, affectionate parents send their children there to sit and sweat a whole summer day, to acquire habits of neatness and order, and a love of knowledge. The long summer days that I have sat in such, upon a hard bench, with a back as straight as a corset, enjoying not only the birds flitting about at liberty, in which was poetry, but even the little pigs wallowing in their filth, are graven upon my memory as with sharp steel; and often, in this State, have I been reminded, by the school houses, of those wretched days.

Chapter Five

The Rural Schoolteacher

Equality in physical environment was not then considered necessary to equality in opportunity. Then, as now, the wealthier communities provided better homes and better equipment for comforts of the children. The rural people exercised greater care in selecting a teacher. They had better opportunity to know more of the personality and habits of each teacher. Their teachers became more nearly a part of the community and of the family. The teacher was more than the subjects she taught.

— William Thomas Carrington, *History of Education in Missouri*

The Geyer Act of 1839 authorized the position of superintendent of common schools, and an 1853 law provided for county commissioners of common schools to set standards for teachers. They were expected to qualify in respect to character, learning, and ability for positions in the public schools, but no license was required. In fact, teachers often were not well trained, for the earliest rural schools were mostly subscription schools with standards set by the parents. Although rural parents did exercise great care in choosing a teacher, their choices were sometimes limited. A fifteen-year-old would be hired simply because she or he had completed the eighth grade and could read, write, "do some figurin'," and was known personally in the community. Males who were not interested in

Most teachers took great pride in taking care of the children they taught, seeing that they were as comfortable as possible in the drafty log cabins. By the
1880s, according to Wayne E. Fuller, a saying among school administrators
was "as is the teacher, so is the school." Otillia Biesemeyer, the teacher at
Winkelmann School near Westphalia in Osage County, smiles proudly in
front of her school. (Courtesy of Earl Lubensky)

becoming farmers, tradesmen, or miners hired themselves out as
teachers. They qualified simply by their interest in reading and
"scholarly" pursuits. Those needing teachers sometimes placed
ads in newspapers. Some came "highly recommended" from a
seminary or academy. It was not unusual for a school to have as
many as three teachers in one year, and interviews might take
place in a field while a board member was hard at work.

Agreements in writing between a teacher and the patrons of
a subscription school were common. Mary L. Hahn records such
a contract in her book *"Bits of History."* Eli Wilson Cowan,
mentioned in the following agreement, was her great-great-
uncle. "A true copy of a School article Commenced on the 14th
of July 1847 in Greenville Township Wayne County Mo. by
Thomas Taylor for six months provided that:"

1st. I thomas taylor promise to teach [the] Children of this Neighborhood to the number of Twenty five if that many can be made up, or will commence with twenty to teach six months at the rate of Two dollars and fifty cents per scholar per quarter or three months. I will teach spelling, reading, writing, the rudiments of arithmetic, . . . simple Interest and compound Interest, also teach the vernacular Language, teach five days in each week and if any time is lost by Thomas Taylor by sickness or otherwise to be made up before the Experation of Teaching.

2nd. We the undersigned employers to this article promise to pay to Thomas Taylor the above sum per scholar on or before the experation of teaching. I will receive Cash, Pork, Beefhides, Deerskins, Mink skins, Raccoon skins or any fur if good, also woolen Jeans Cloth, shirting cloth or Young Cattle one year not over, a young Beef Steer or Cow. The defirent articles as above to be delivered me at Mr. Eli Cowans on or before the experation. The Schoolhouse to be Comfortable fixed with a good roof writing Tables or Benches. Also seats Benches to sit on. Fuel furnished when needed.

Mary Hahn goes on to say, "Judging from the spelling, punctuation, wording and arrangement of the 'contract' one would wonder just how much a child could learn."

In 1836, Reverend Martin D. Noland agreed to the following rules while teaching in a subscription school in Cole County.

The ones that come first in the morning say first. (recite)

No scholar will be allowed to swear or make use of any profane language.

There will not be allowed any swinging, wrestling, quarreling or fighting among any of the scholars.

No scholar will be allowed to tag, nickname or make fun of the clothing of any other scholar.

When any person not belonging to the school comes into the school house the scholars will rise from their seats and make a gentle bow.

Large scholars will be allowed no more privileges than small ones.

The boys and girls will not be allowed to play together.

The scholars will not be allowed to cut or grease the benches.

There shall be but one go out at any time without permission.

No scholar will be allowed to go out more than twice after play time without permission.

School rules the teacher was expected to enforce also covered going to and from school. Hickory County rules stated: "There shall be no going into any person's orchard or melon patch without the consent of the owner. No pupil is allowed to carry firearms or play cards or carry cards to school." Maries County ruled: "No calling names or swearing on the road. No quarreling or fighting on the road. No throwing stones at one another on the road. No playing on the road, especially tag. No carrying articles home belonging to the school and no leaving gates open on the road." The last rule was important because leaving gates open allowed livestock to get loose. A school rule in 1847 simply stated: "Come to school at half past 7:00 and come with clean hands and face and hair combed."

Female teachers could not marry. If one did, it would be the end of her professional teaching career. Texas County rules for teachers in 1872 stated, "Women teachers who marry or engage in unseemly conduct will be dismissed" and most county officials had similar rules. As late as 1907 *The Odessan* of Lafayette County published "Why Married Women Should Not Teach" by William Garrison, former president of the Boston School Committee.

Some townships and subscription patrons told teachers how to handle their money. "Every teacher should lay aside from each pay a goodly sum of his earnings for his benefit . . . so he will not become a burden on society." Some were told what to read: "The Bible will be read every evening for an hour" or "After ten hours in school, the teachers may spend the remaining time reading the Bible or other good books." Since country schools were also the center of social activities, the teachers were expected to plan social affairs in addition to their daily teaching duties. This meant being in continual contact with their students. Those who felt comfortable with the constant scrutiny and socializing became an important part of the community.

Most counties held the teacher's warrant (paycheck) until the monthly report was made to the county school superintendent, listing scholars in attendance that month. Some received part of their wages from subscription parents and the rest from local school funds. Records show that in the 1840s Washington School District, six miles north of Paris, Missouri, paid teachers $20.00 to $35.00 a month. Teachers in the Ozark regions taught for $0.25 a day. By 1850, Independence School in Dallas County paid teachers $23.50 a month. Eckler School in Montgomery County paid teachers $30.00 a month for teaching two months in 1870. As late as the 1880s, Franklin School in Clay County paid teachers $35.00 for a summer term of three months and $45.00 for a winter term lasting six months. At Blooming Rose, a rural subscription school on the Pulaski/Texas county line that George M. Reed attended from 1880 to 1883, one dollar a month was paid for boys and fifty cents for girls.

Teachers often faced problems in carrying out their duties. Children on the Missouri frontier had a spirit of independence. Older students carried guns and knives, which resulted in occasional injury. Maintaining control was especially difficult for a woman or a meek male teacher. The "mean-spirited" boys would taunt, tease, and even pick up the teacher. Since rural schools were isolated, the teacher had no one to help when scholars, many of them bigger and stronger than the teacher, got out of control. Many capable teachers were "run off" by the students.

Parents were sometimes as spirited as their children. An article in A History of the Pioneer Families of Missouri tells of a Frenchman named Peter Conoier living on Marais Croche Lake in St. Charles County in 1827:

> One of his sons, named Joseph, while going to school, was chastised by the teacher, for some misdemeanor, and the old gentleman was greatly incensed thereat. He determined to

whip the teacher in turn and went to the school house next morning for that purpose. Arriving at the school house, he drew his knife out and began to whet it on his foot, whereupon the teacher drew *his* knife, and invited him to "come on," if that were his game. But concluding that discretion was the better part of valor, he put up his knife, bade the teacher a polite good morning, and went home.

Physical punishment was the solution many teachers used for difficult discipline problems. A teacher needed an air of authority or "backbone" to keep control, and a switch or paddle was one way to handle unruly students. Parents usually supported the teacher. Some families followed the rule, "If you get a lickin' at school, you'll get another one at home." A California, Missouri, teacher must have known she would have the support of the family when she wrote a note to another teacher, "Emmitt confessed. I am going with him to his father's tonight and preach to him." Miss Nola Thomas, while teaching at Lamine, visited a student's house and told the parents, "I had to switch John today. He kept crawling around under the seats."

Teachers devised many ways to keep order. Discipline varied from teacher to teacher. If a student chewed gum in class, a teacher might make the student tie it to his or her nose with twine and keep it there all day. One teacher in Lawrence County cut letters from newspapers and forced students with spelling difficulties to eat them. A typical punishment was writing "I will never _____ again" one hundred times on the blackboard. Two unruly students might have their heads knocked together. Some rural teachers drew a circle on the blackboard and made the offender stand with nose pressed against the board in that circle. A child might be made to sit or stand in the corner or be whacked across the knuckles with a ruler or stick. Boys were sometimes made to wear sunbonnets and sit with the girls. In Montgomery County, a rural teacher wore a heavy gold ring on her finger and knocked "troublemakers" on the head with it.

A successful way to deal with discipline problems was to hire a female teacher in the spring for the younger children while older scholars were working in the fields, and then hire a male teacher during the winter months to handle the big boys. Some school boards expected male teachers to keep order first and perhaps teach a little as well. Will Edwards, the clerk of Maries County, and Bridge Briggs, a teacher, declared that "if these rules are violated, The Pupil will be Punished By Being whipped or Standing on the floor and if Pupil refuses to Being whipped or standing on floore, they Shall Be Expelled from school." Standing on the floor meant not being able to sit for a period of time.

A child who was tardy might get a whipping or might be locked out of school and have to wait outside no matter what the weather until the teacher decided what punishment fit the misconduct. Even worse for some was having to return home and report to their family that they had been tardy.

It was common for teachers to board with the parents of their students. In *History of Lafayette County Missouri Rural Schools*, Virginia Lee Slusher Fisher remembers that when she attended Garr School in Lafayette County her teacher boarded in her home. "For five years, Miss Ella Carter was our teacher. Stern of countenance, black braids pinned around her head, she was not to be taken lightly. Besides, she lived at our house and that is a special kind of burden for a youngster. You can't talk to your folks about how mean the teacher is. You know any misbehavior will be reported before you have a chance."

Teachers and children got to school as best they could in rural areas. Debbie Hefner described in the *Waynesville Daily Guide* how Irene Bowling made her winter trips to a one-room schoolhouse in the Ozarks:

> Bowling rode a horse seven miles to and from the school, and said at times the journey would be dangerous in the middle of the winter. "I would wear a long riding skirt over a heavy dress and underwear, and with all the layers of clothes, I needed help getting on and off the horse," she said. "When it was cold, I couldn't stop at a neighbor's house and warm up, because I wouldn't be able to get back on again."

Rural Schools of Dallas County includes Raymond Gott's memories of one of his teachers who got lost in a snowstorm:

> In the early schools it was almost unheard of for a teacher to miss even one day of school. Blanche Pendergraft, the teacher at that time, was attempting to reach Mt. Harmony [School] by foot in a blinding snow storm. She was following an almost submerged fence line as her guide, [but] became confused and disoriented in the blizzard. A neighbor, Bill Jackson, happened to see the situation and went after her. Had it not been for his help, she surely would have become hopelessly lost and probably would have frozen.

In an unpublished essay by Peggy Scott in the collections of the State Historical Society of Missouri, R. Glen Jones, who taught at the rural Stroderville School in Whitewater, recalls students coming to school "through rain, snow, ice, cold, or hot. . . . Some of the kids looked like little snowmen when they got to school. Their cheeks would be rosy-red and their eyes bright as buttons."

A minimum attendance was required to keep a school open. Mike Price, a German who settled in St. Charles County, assured one man of his teaching position that school term, as *A History of the Pioneer Families of Missouri* relates:

> Mike had married and in about twenty years . . . had twelve children, and he surprised the district school master one morning by presenting himself at the door of the school house with nine of them to be placed under his charge. He said he would have brought three more, but their mother hadn't finished their clothes. They were promptly on hand next morning, and increased the number of pupils to respectable proportions.

Sister Marie Lamb attended Aud School in Benton County and remembers, "When I started the first grade I had six siblings in the same room." One family of brothers, sisters, and cousins might make up an entire class enrollment. On occasion, when a large family moved the school the children had been attending was forced to close.

In a report to the twentieth Missouri General Assembly in 1858, W. B. Starke, the state superintendent of common schools, encouraged the establishment of normal schools, that is, schools to train teachers. "The influence of the Normal School is at once to elevate the character of both teachers and schools, and to induce amongst the people a better, higher and nobler sentiment on the subject of popular education. Wherever a permanent school is established by a competent and faithful teacher, it becomes a focus of light."

By the mid-1800s the state required teaching certificates. County institutes provided two-week courses semiannually for teachers. Certificates were valid only in the county where they were issued. There were three grades of certificates—first, second, and third. The third-grade certification, valid for one year, was awarded when a candidate correctly answered 80 percent of the test questions. The second-grade certification was for two years and required that 85 percent of the questions be answered correctly, while the first-grade certification was valid for three years when 90 percent of the questions were answered correctly.

County institutes were the forerunner of the state normal colleges in Missouri. The first regional normal school was established in Kirksville in 1867, followed by schools in Warrensburg in 1871 and Cape Girardeau in 1873. Lincoln Institute in Jefferson City had started with two students in 1866 but had seventeen by the third day of classes. In 1870, through the efforts of black leaders and other supporters, the legislature and governor approved a resolution providing $5,000 annually to Lincoln to train teachers, and in 1879 it became a state-supported school. George R. Smith College for Negroes, established by the Freedmen's Aid and Southern Education Society of the Methodist Episcopal Church, opened in Sedalia in January 1894 with an enrollment of fifty-seven students. According to Rose Nolen, who wrote a history of the college, George R. Smith had graduated more than three thousand students, many of them teachers, before it was destroyed by fire

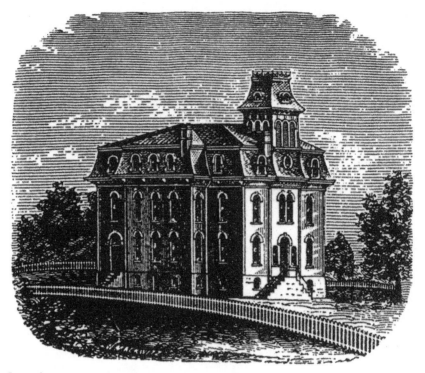

Lincoln Institute began in an abandoned schoolhouse on Hobo Hill in Jefferson City. In 1871 it was able to erect its first building on the site of today's campus. The historian Antonio Holland wrote, "The famous black leader W. E. B. Du Bois once said that Lincoln Institute 'had perhaps the most romantic beginning of all the black colleges.' DuBois was correct, for Lincoln University began in the hearts and minds of a small group of black soldiers, fighting the odds and molding a dream of a better future for themselves and generations to come." Lincoln Institute became Lincoln University in 1921. (Lincoln Collection, Inman E. Page Library, Lincoln University, Jefferson City)

in 1925. Normal schools in Maryville and Springfield were founded in 1905.

Some of the normal schools had more support than others. In *History of Lincoln University*, William Sherman Savage explains, "Normal schools at that time covered a 'multitude of sins.' They were not strictly teacher-training schools. Such institutions that were not public and had not reached the place where they could be called colleges, were designated as Normal schools or Universities, whether there was any reason for it or not." Progress was not always smooth, but the normal schools continued to develop. They applied standardized methods, tested and evaluated new theories, and gradually helped to eliminate the unfit teacher from the teaching profession.

Teaching all ages, from first grade through eighth grade, in a one-room school, the teacher spread literacy, persevering until most children could read, speak and write in English, spell, and calculate numbers. Boys and girls coming from different nationalities and backgrounds began the process of learning to live in a common culture. The conscientious teacher kept lessons prepared, the floor swept, and a fire burning on cold days.

The determined teacher worked toward the progress of each child and felt personally rewarded on seeing them achieve. A favorite expression of one determined teacher was, "Good lessons and good order." The devout teacher read from the Bible each day and led the class in reciting the Lord's Prayer. Buck Sisson of Joplin, Missouri, was expected to memorize a verse listing the books of the Old Testament and still remembers many of the stanzas:

> In Genesis the world was made,
> In Exodus the march is told,
> Leviticus contains the Law,
> In Numbers are the tribes enrolled.
> . . . .
> Then Zachariah speaks of Christ,
> And Malachi of John his sign,
> The Prophets number seventeen,
> And all the books are thirty-nine.

The sympathetic teacher treated tears with tenderness, wasp stings with salve, cuts with bandages, and frostbitten fingers and toes with warmth. In *History of Lafayette County Missouri Rural Schools*, Mary Kirchhoff, a teacher at Centerview School District 2, recalls, "We always had needles, thread, thimble and buttons on hand for repairs of all kinds, both boys and girls needed them at times." One hygiene-conscious teacher at Two Mile School in Oregon County had the students line up before lunch. She went down the line pouring melted hand soap from a jar into their cupped hands. Another student followed with a bucket of water and a long-handled dipper, pouring water over the students' hands to rinse off the soap. Lucy Willett, who taught in Cedar County, saw to it that the "poorer children didn't miss out on their education for lack of shoes or lunch." She solicited contributions of clothing from merchants and also bought many items herself.

The caring teacher protected the children against flooding creeks, rabid animals, and thunderstorms and calmed their fears when a Native American peered through the window or gypsies camped in covered wagons in the school yard. Railroad tracks ran by Goss School near Paris, Missouri. Sometimes the teacher and students arrived at school to find hobos sleeping inside. Lou B. Callis, who attended that school, said, "No harm ever came of it—but it did frighten us. The hobos kept the fire going at night making the school warm in the morning."

Edna Lee Webb Stalling described her experience at Harris School in *History of Lafayette County Missouri Rural Schools*:

> One afternoon at three o'clock, a storm came up. Black clouds tumbled over the corn field in surges, and winds howled from every direction. Shouting at the top of my voice, I called all the children inside. It was getting very dark, and it took the combined strength of the older boys and my own to get the big front doors closed and bolted. The children went at once to their seats and hung on as gusts shook the building. They sang songs and told jokes taking turns. Riddles followed jokes, as children eagerly waited their turn. By now, water was creeping up the seat supports and pupils placed their feet in the iron circles [at the base of each desk] as they stood to recite. I will never forget the rosy, curly-haired little fifth grader who loved riddles better than anything and gleefully called "Give Up?" above the roar of wind and water.

Some playful teachers joined in the children's games. Mildred McCormack, who taught at King's Point School, north of Thayer, remembers the time she let the children bury her in leaves. She warned the children to let her know if anyone came by. The county commissioner showed up unexpectedly. When she popped up out of the leaves, she saw him and said, "Oh, my God." Mildred heard one student say, "Was she prayin' or a cussin'?" Mrs. Carl Baldwin, a former rural teacher now living in Vienna, Missouri, said, "When it snowed, I eliminated the second recess and had one and a half hours at lunch so we could slide." She was sixteen years old at the time and went sliding with the children.

The creative teacher instilled the joy of discovery and self-expression in the children. A teacher in Dallas County did just that, as reported in *Rural Schools of Dallas County:*

> Another interesting thing which happened on the first Friday afternoon of that term, was the arrival of several parents some thirty to forty minutes before classes were to conclude for the day. They told me they had just come early to "visit school." As the term progressed and I realized this was to be a regular event, I decided this would be a good time for the children to share some things they had learned—in a creative manner. They presented a few little plays based on stories which they read or on stories I read to them daily after lunch. Songs learned in music class and poems were shared. Some of their art work was displayed. The parents and students seemed to look forward to this time. I noticed the children's confidence increased as time passed.

The patient teacher taught the virtues of listening and reasoning. Jean Everling of Holt remembers her grandfather, Emmett Templeton Hollingshead, a teacher in Putnam County, telling her how he started each school day. He instructed the children to "THINK—about all the things you know. LISTEN—to everything going on around you. ABSORB—take in everything you hear and see. THINK again—put all you have heard and seen in

order and add to what you already know. And RESPOND—
share your collected knowledge with others appropriately."

Marvin Thomas, who was both a student and a teacher in a
one-room schoolhouse, believes, "one of the stronger points of
a rural school was that teachers could give individual instruction and any child could participate in any grade level."

In Norma Lea (Anderson) Mihalevich's family, being a
teacher became a family tradition, as reported in *Pulaski County
Rural Schools:*

> My father . . . taught 25 years in Pulaski County Schools. . . .
> [in] Laquey, Pleasant Grove, Shockley, Fairview, Cedar
> Hill, Crocker and Dublin. . . . Mother, Laura Walters
> Anderson, . . . taught at Prospect and Pleasant Grove.
> Mother always instilled in all of us the great rewards in
> teaching. . . . My sister Mildred . . . and I both taught at the
> Rolling Heath School located across the Piney River. . . .
> Marjorie (Anderson) Bandy taught at the Anderson
> School and the Waynesville School. . . . My brother Earl
> Anderson taught 50 years in the same school in Williams-
> burg, Kansas. . . . My sister Neva (Anderson) Ramsey
> taught one year in 1930. . . . In the extended family of Ora
> and Laura Anderson there are seven more grandchildren
> who are teaching, or have taught at sometime in their
> lives. . . . The profession of teaching as far as our family is
> concerned was and is a noble profession. To touch the life
> of a child and direct them in a good and successful life
> enriches our [own] in a tremendous way.

Chapter Six

The Scholars' Day

We went to Possumtown through rain storms and blizzards. My father, bless him, would get up early and make a path through the snow for us. My dear mother would massage our hands and feet when we returned home. Discipline was heavy and the teacher was always right, even though my father asked for fairness from the teacher and the truth from his children.

— Bobby Flock, *Osage County Historical Society Newsletter*

The child "scholars" often had to tend to chores before leaving for school. Sometimes older children helped dress and feed their younger brothers and sisters. When the chores were done, it was time to wash up under the pump or from a bucket of water, pack a lunch, and start out for school. In *Pulaski County Rural Schools*, Frank Case tells about his mornings before going to Needmore School:

Dad and I would go outside and do our morning chores. We had to feed the horses, pigs, chickens and feed and milk the cows. . . . By the time we had the chores done and had come inside, Mom would have cooked breakfast on the wood stove. . . . We always had homemade biscuits and gravy with butter that Mom had churned from sweet cream and homemade jelly made from berries or fruit she had

picked. We only had eggs when the hens were laying good
and meat at butchering time in the fall and winter.

Lunch was often leftovers from breakfast, but the food varied
depending on the family's economic circumstances. Biscuits or
corn bread filled with hard-fried eggs, bits of bacon, some ham
or sausage or molasses and butter, thin slices of fried mush or
deep-fried potatoes, and in some seasons a piece of meat from a
home-cured rabbit, squirrel, raccoon, or deer were packed in
molasses tins or pokes (paper sacks) or wrapped up in cloth to
take to school. Fresh fruit such as apples, peaches, or strawberries
might be picked on the way to and from school.

Chicken was a rare treat. In *The History of Rural Schools of
Putnam County, 1843–1965*, a teacher from Friendship School
describes what happened one day when two sisters brought
chicken for lunch. The older girl wanted everyone to know they
had chicken. She called loudly to her the sister, "If you want
your piece of 'chicking' you had of thee better come and get it."
Gladys Handley of Plattsburg said, "Sometimes I'd have a boiled
egg and I'd have to take a little piece of newspaper and put some
salt on it and fold it real careful so it wouldn't spill. Mother
always had biscuits. I'd take a biscuit." Homer Croy wrote in
Country Cured that at noon, when he opened his dinner bucket,
"there would be a package with grease spots showing through
the brown paper—a delicious cold sausage cake."

Irene Bradley Bennett attended the Pattersonville school in
Dallas County and remembers that "in the fall we would have
grapes, apples, pears or peaches. In winter, with the stove heat-
ing the room, the teacher would cook dry beans or make veg-
etable soup. What a treat!" Students sometimes found holes in
their sacks where mice had nibbled. One Oregon County
scholar recalled that his mother "always put a cup of gravy in my
lunch bucket." When it froze solid, he pretended it was ice
cream and "watched the mouths of other students water."
Swapping food at lunchtime was as popular then as it is today.

Most children walked to school. During soaking rains and
freezing weather the roads and paths were almost impassable.

A typical school day started at 4:00 a.m. with children getting up to help with the morning chores; eat breakfast; gather their lunch, books, and slates; and start out to school, often while it was still dark. (State Historical Society of Missouri, Columbia)

Droves of cattle, horses, buggies, and wagons made deep ruts in the roads. Walking in wet clay and mud in Missouri is often compared to walking in chewing gum. Mud stuck to the children's shoes, which grew heavier and heavier as more and more mud collected. Often in bad weather, children preferred going barefoot, carrying their shoes until they got to school. Teachers recalled seeing blood in the snow from children's bare feet, and many kept a clean cloth and turpentine available to bandage cuts and treat stubbed toes.

It was not uncommon for pairs of shoes to be shared in a family. This often left one or more members without shoes. According to *The History of Rural Schools of Putnam County*, Emanual Parker, while attending Medicineville School 13 in York Township in 1863, thought of an unusual way to keep his bare feet from freezing:

Father made our shoes. The older ones got their shoes first so they could do chores. I was the third boy, so sometimes it got plenty frosty weather before I got mine. I had a nice smooth oak board that I would set up by the old fireplace, get it right hot, put it under my arm and start out frosty mornings barefooted to school, one and one-fourth miles. My feet would get so cold I would lay my board down, jump on it to warm my feet, then make another trot toward school.

Shoes might be made from the hide of a deer, squirrel, or sometimes a cat and tied with a cord, like moccasins. The leather was often tanned at home. That could take up to eighteen months, but when winter arrived and shoes were needed, the leather was cut and shaped even though it was only half-tanned. Untanned leather swelled, stretched, and crawled off the wearer's feet when wet. As it dried, it shrank and fitted so tight it caused blisters and cuts. One remembered that "many a poor boy and girl raised a squall at the idea of putting on their shoes when their feet and ankles were sore because of cuts and bruises from those rawhide shoes."

Shortcuts were commonplace when students lived several miles from the schoolhouse. The scholars might cut through an orchard, circle a farmhouse, crawl under a fence, or follow a rail around a springhouse to a bridge. Their shortcuts took them through tall prairie grasses and low-water creek beds, all the time having to watch for snakes and poison ivy. If the water in a creek was high, they "cooned a log" by walking across on a fallen tree. They faced the danger of being attacked by a rabid animal, a pack of wild dogs, coyotes, bears, or sometimes even an angry bull or range cow in a farmer's field.

Nature caused most of the problems as the students walked to and from school, but other students could cause problems as well. At any time a scholar could be bombarded with snowballs, acorns, peaches, pawpaws, persimmons, or green walnuts. With no one nearby to help, the victims had to defend themselves or outrun their attacker.

Most children walked to school, but some were lucky enough to get there by horseback. All ages and sizes of scholars attended the one-room school. Sometimes the older ones came only long enough to learn to write their names, and sometimes children not yet of school age accompanied a brother or sister to school. (State Historical Society of Missouri, Columbia)

On snowy days, Nadine Cansler's father walked ahead of the children and broke a path for them in deep snow. In Newton County, bigger boys would help by dragging a fence rail to break a trail for the girls. A farmer could remove the wheels from his wagon, put on runners, and take children to school on a makeshift sleigh. When Christmas season arrived, a set of sleigh bells on the horses added to the fun, usually resulting in a round of Christmas carols being sung on the way. But most were not as fortunate. Ralph Hooker, who attended Washington School in Carthage, walked four miles. When the snow was deep his mother tied gunnysacks over his shoes and legs to keep them from being frostbitten.

Girls' school clothes changed over the years. A common style in the early 1800s was a yarn linsey-woolsey dress spun from wool and flax with a calico or checked gingham apron buttoned over it to keep it clean, since often girls had only one dress. These dresses have been described as being "as plain as a night-gown." Girls wore wool hose and long underwear in the winter. Gladys Handley remembers, "We wore long underwear and I did hate that stuff. You had to fold it over down at the ankle and pull your stocking up quick so you wouldn't pull the underwear up, too." Crochet hoods or sunbonnets were sometimes worn throughout the year. Patches were sewn on worn-out dresses passed down from older sisters. In the late 1800s, feed sacks came in stripes, paisley prints, and checks and were cut up and sewn into "school clothes."

Boys might wear homespun jeans or buckskin pants, a hickory-dyed homespun cotton shirt or one made of feed sacking, and cowhide boots or cobbling boots, as those made by a cobbler were called. Their hats were knit or wide brimmed to resemble their fathers' hats. Patches were also common on boys' bib overalls or pants inherited from older brothers. If the pants were two sizes too big, galluses (suspenders) were used to hold them up.

Distinctive odors greeted the children each day as they opened the door to their one-room schoolhouse. The close quarters led to a variety of smells. Children did not take baths daily throughout most of the nineteenth century. Strong body odors and odors from wearing the same soiled clothes day after day mingled with the smell of livestock manure and decaying plants that was absorbed into their shoes.

During winter months, a boy or girl sometimes wore a necklace of garlic or an asafetida bag tied with a string around the neck to ward off colds and flu. Those cloth bags held herbs and strong smelling gum resin. The odor was so strong it stung noses and could make eyes tear up. The smell of goose grease also lingered in the schoolhouse during those coldest months of the year. Goose grease was rubbed on chests to loosen congestion from a cold.

Boys might check the traps they had set for raccoons or beavers on their way to school. If they caught a skunk, their clothes reeked from the odor and they were most often sent home to change. The piercing smell of wet unwashed wool from mittens, scarves, and coats drying by the fire in combination with other strong odors caused many teachers to keep a window or the school door open on even the coldest days.

There were also pleasant smells in the schoolhouse. Wooden floors, cleaned the night before, gave off the lingering smell of oiled sawdust. Wood burning in the fireplace or wood stove had a strong pleasant smell, reminding children of their own homes. After recess on a cold snowy day, the teacher might surprise her students with a hot apple cider treat or hot chocolate. In the spring, students picked wildflowers and brought them to school to be placed on the teacher's desk. Those sweet smells filled the room, accompanied by the buzzing of the bees that followed the blossoms indoors.

Having arrived safely, the students began their typical school day with a prayer and a reading from the Bible. After 1892, some teachers had the children recite the Pledge of Allegiance to the flag. There was roll call and sometimes a patriotic song. The students might sing "The Star-Spangled Banner" or "Battle Hymn of the Republic." Ralph L. Hooker sang this song every morning:

> Good morning merry sunshine
> How do you wake so soon?
> You frightened all the stars away
> and drive away the moon.

Teachers inspected students' nails, hair, teeth, and hands to make sure they were clean. And each student, one by one, stuck out his or her tongue so the teacher could inspect for a red throat indicating infection. Awards were given at the end of the year to the children who had not missed any school days and passed health inspection every morning.

Some schools had a long recitation bench at the front of the room. When it was the turn for each grade to recite, the teacher might say, "Geography class. Rise and Pass!" The students rushed to the bench to get a place to sit. If there were too many to fit on the bench, the "latecomers" stood during the entire recitation. Some teachers drew a recitation line on the floor. Those reciting placed their toes on the line and stood facing the teacher. In a school in Montgomery County, the teacher had a single row of nails twelve inches apart on the raised platform. Students stood with their toes on the nails, forming a straight

The teacher had the children read aloud or recite in turn. (State Historical Society of Missouri, Columbia)

line facing the class. Groups took turns reciting while others studied their assigned lessons.

Until the state published its "Course of Study" in the 1850s, the choice of subjects was decided by the county superintendents and county commissioners of common schools. In some early schools, the students read through six readers. This completed their education. There were few records of progress. Even if a term or two was missed, a student could return and begin all over. It was often said that "no one ever finishes a country school."

In "The Bates Tribe," a memoir by Hugh Latham Bates of Monroe County, he recalls his early school experience:

> That fall, at age seven, I started to school in Wafer Ash School, just three-quarters of a mile from home. It was no shock, for I already knew a good many of the students, or scholars, as they were erroneously called. Father took me the first day and stayed until he was sure I was going to

stay too. The teacher was a man, Mr. Cauthern, and, as I recall, a good average teacher. It took him about a week to discover that I had been exposed to about everything in the first grade, so he put me in second, to the surprise and dismay of some of my compatriots who knew very well that this was my first year in school. Mother had done all right by me.

The students' school day largely depended on the teacher's philosophy. A theory of the time was "no licking; no learning." Whipping with a sapling switch made from a small branch was the most frequently used punishment. The teacher's switches were in plain view of the scholars, and if a switch was not available, the teacher sent someone out to cut switches with the warning not to notch them or he would be switched, too. Scholars knew that if the switch was notched it would break easily, saving a friend or sibling from further punishment. In the Ozarks, getting whipped with a peach-tree switch was known as "peach-tree tea." An old Ozark folk song tells of "hickory tea":

> Still sits the schoolhouse by the road
> Close by the old oak tree,
> Where many a boy has took a dose
> Of grim old hickory tea

In an article in *Gateway Heritage*, Lisa Heffernan shared the remembrance of Minnie Willet of Callaway County about a teacher so strict "you'd be afraid to tear a sheet of paper off of your tablet because it'd make a little bit of noise, or if you were to drop your pencil on the floor, you'd have to stand up in the corner." "Sassing" the teacher could bring trouble because most parents supported the teacher. Behind the parent was the school board, and it was always understood that the county superintendent would paddle a misbehaving student if necessary.

An article in *The Era of the One-Room Rural Schools of Cedar County, Missouri* describes one boy's experience:

Don had only been in school a few days when he felt the sting of one of Bill Brown's clubs. As a little brother with three older sisters, Don saw nothing wrong in doing as he did at home, so when his sister's long hair flowed back over his desk top, he braided it. His sister thought nothing of it either. But as Mr. Brown patrolled the room without saying a word, he brought the six foot club down across the surprised boy's hand.

Lillie Jackson attended Walnut Grove School in Stone County. *The History of Stone County, Missouri,* includes her recollection of a group switching in her school:

> One incident I well remember happened when my brother, Duton Langley, was teaching. One morning he told us, "Today there will be no whispering." At the last recess he brought in several switches from small to large. Then he said for everyone who had whispered to line up in front of the room. Max Spears was visiting that day so he went forward with the rest of us and took his whipping. There were 27 kids in that line. You may well believe that the next day when he said, "Don't whisper," we didn't whisper!

Over the years, paddling with a board eventually replaced whipping with a switch. As one Ozark resident explained, "They (the little ones) didn't need it after he'd (the teacher) busted (thrashed) a few of them big 'uns, the little 'uns didn't do it anymore." So even those earliest harsh methods of discipline may have influenced some of the "little ones" of the next generation.

Recess was always a favorite part of the school day—a time to play and socialize. In the earliest schools, nature supplied the "equipment." There were cornfields in which to play hide-and-seek and caves for all kinds of make-believe adventures. If there wasn't a cave, children might dig one out in a hillside. Nearby creeks had an abundance of crawdads to chase and rocks for building dams. Swinging on grapevines hanging from trees provided hours of fun. Gladys Handley of Plattsburg and her friends

Teachers on the frontier often resorted to the "hickory stick," and children sometimes made up derogatory rhymes or chants. One recorded by Vance Randolph shows the students' dislike of the teacher:

> The devil flew from north to south
> And caught old Wesley by the mouth
> But when he found he was such a fool
> He left him here to teach our school

made up a game called "bear." The bear stood in a ditch and tried to catch players as they crossed over. Play could include a creative game such as doodlebug, made up by children in Montgomery County. Ant lions, or doodlebugs, lived in loose dirt under their school. They repeated "doodle up" until a bug appeared and "doodle down" until it disappeared.

Girls made play houses out of pebbles and sticks and sweet clover or straw. Sometimes they were allowed to bring homemade dolls to school. Some dolls consisted of cloth stuffed with rags or sawdust. Cornhusk dolls and corncob dolls had corn silk

Recess was the best part of the day for most students. They made up games, recited counting-out rhymes, and sometimes shouted rhymes about their teacher: "Teacher, teacher, I declare / I see bedbugs in your hair" and "Peanuts and jellycake / Teacher's got a bellyache" are two collected by Vance Randolph. (State Historical Society of Missouri, Columbia)

fashioned into hair, beards, and mustaches. "Leaving dolls" were made from material "leavings" or scraps left over after a sewing project. Fabric was scarce and expensive. Other homemade dolls were constructed from burlap, flour sacks, rope, or wildflowers and had faces drawn with berry juice or charcoal. Tops of acorns and shells were play dishes. The girls made bracelets and neck-laces from pine needles and flowering weeds.

Boys made wigwams out of saplings fastened together at the top with a carpet of leaves inside. Saplings were also used as a seesaw by pulling them down and sitting on them. When the sapling was released it tossed the rider across the school yard. This is an account of one student's experience:

> We would often bend down a sapling, a half dozen or more crawl on and take a free ride, see-saw fashion. On this fateful day during the last recess we were see-sawing away in great style when the school bell rang. We all jumped off to go to lessons, but a projecting knot on the tree in its upward swing caught me in the most vulnerable part of my knee-trousers and every seam was ripped out. Imagine if you can my mortification.

Boys "wrassled." That was a favorite recess activity, although some teachers didn't permit it because it could get too rough and cause injury. Mumblety-peg was another popular boy's game. A knife was tossed from various positions, and points were given when the blade stuck in the ground. Scholars living in rural areas carried pocket knives for a multitude of reasons.

Typical outdoor games included drop the handkerchief, leapfrog, crack the whip, farmer in the dell, ring-around-the-rosy, London bridge, and blindman's buff. Everyone competed in racing and relays. Children played "ante over" until the ball they were playing with, made from a sock or strips of rags, unwound and the walnut or hickory nut at the center fell out. Marbles were often made by baking balls of clay; if the school had a dirt floor, a variety of marble games were played inside.

Winter games included ice-skating if a nearby pond was frozen. Wayne Wolfe attended Victor School, originally named Compton Hill, in Crawford County and wrote for the newsletter of the Osage County Historical Society about his experience while playing on ice:

> One very cold winter day a group of us were playing on the ice, and a thin spot broke beneath me. I fell through and went under the ice, and since the other boys had some trouble breaking through and rescuing me, my clothes froze stiff. I had to be carried part of the way to the schoolhouse.

> The teacher placed a curtain across one corner of the room and made me take off all my clothes so they could be dried by the fire. I had to sit behind the curtain with all the other students just on the other side . . . how embarrassing!

Students and teachers played fox and geese, and many a teacher and student had their faces washed in the snow or lost a snow-ball fight.

A favorite traditional game played by several generations of rural schoolchildren was needle's eye. Two children held hands, stretching them up to form an arch. The players passed through the arch while moving in a circle singing:

> The needle's eye
> That doth supply,
> The thread that runs so true;
> Many a beau, have I let go,
> Because I wanted you.
> Many a dark and stormy night,
> When I went home with you,
> I stumped my toe and down I go,
> Because I wanted you.

The arch came down over the player who passed through on the last "you." The ones forming the arch took each captured child aside and asked the same question. A question might be, "Do you want to be a hard-boiled egg or a soft-boiled egg?" The answer determined which side the player would be on in a game of tug-of-war.

After recess, it was once again "time for books." Fridays usu-ally ended with spelling bees or geography hunts or ciphering matches with everyone competing to be considered the best speller or mathematician in the school. As it grew dark in bad weather, some parents came after their scholars on horseback or in a wagon or buggy.

Pranks and mischief were common. George Harman and his brother Fred, who attended Buckendorf School in Osage

County, caught a mouse that came up through a hole in the floor. As he reported in the newsletter of the county's historical society, "They tied a string around its leg, released it to run back down the hole, then yanked it back just as it almost disappeared through the floor. All the pupils were ready to burst with laughter, while the teacher was unaware for quite some time as to the cause of the merriment." Betty Collum Harrison, who attended Gore School in Warren County, recalls that some pranksters would fast-forward the clock on the teacher's desk in hopes of going home sooner. A favorite of many mischief makers was to tell frightening stories on the way to school about a wildcat being seen in the area. After school, they hid behind bushes and made sounds like a wildcat until everyone ran in fear.

Sometimes a loud pop exploded from acorns or shot that someone had put in the school fireplace or stove. Buckeye explosions sounded like a shotgun. Gladys Handley recalls the time some boys in her school threw shot at the blackboard to hear it explode and how they got in trouble:

> The teacher lined all seven boys up and searched them to find shot in their clothes. They faced the blackboard with their hands behind their backs. While the teacher searched, the rest of us watched the boys pass shot down from one to the other just ahead of the teacher. When it got to the last boy, he swallowed the shot.

Gladys went on to say, "I didn't ever know what happened to that boy . . . if he got sick from the shot."

Most schools at one time or another "turned the teacher out." The school board sometimes gave permission for a "lockout." Christmas was the favored time. Scholars locked or bolted the door so the teacher couldn't get in. The door stayed closed until the scholars received candy or a gift from the teacher. Sue Alexander wrote in *Ray County Reflections* about a teacher who arrived at school to find that she was locked out:

She was determined she was not going to treat again since she had treated at Christmas. . . . so taking the situation in hand, she backed up a long way and made a run for the door, all hundred pounds of her, and the door gave way to reveal not only the entire student body, but three school board members. She said she just walked over and rang the bell and said, "School is now in session." No treats that time!

In *Vienna Centennial, Maries County, Missouri*, J. G. Hutchinson, a student in one of the earliest schools in the area, Bourbois, wrote about a strike on Christmas Day, which in early years was a school day:

It was a favorite diversion of the inmates of these "ruby founts of knowledge" to inaugurate a sort of "strike" on Christmas Day and order the "master" to treat the school, with the tacit understanding that it would be much more pleasant for all concerned than for them to be under the painful necessity of "ducking" his pedagogic highness under the cold ice of the neighboring river. The more conciliatory teacher generally secured enough apples to go round.

Rural Education and Rural Life in Missouri, published by the Missouri Department of Education in 1945, concluded:

The mingling of all ages of boys and girls in the same schoolroom and on the same playground, the long walks to and from school in all kinds of weather, the home chores that must be done before and after school hours develop a resourcefulness and a spirit of independence rarely equalled among urban school children. All these influences combine to establish a steadfastness of purpose and habits of work which make for stability and success.

Chapter Seven

Tools of Learning

The school on each evening closed by the students standing in a line and spelling the words as they were given out by the teacher. Ten minutes were given to get the spelling lesson and as the announcement was made every boy and girl got his blue-back book and spelled aloud with all his might and they could easily be heard a quarter of a mile away.
— H. M. Boyd in *History of Jasper County*

The earliest schools had few supplies. Most learning tools were brought from home. Before paper was available, children wrote with charcoal on large pieces of birch-tree bark. Later, scholars used small individual slates and slate pencils, which were cylinders of rock. These "pencils" were eventually replaced by chalk. Since there were no desks in the earliest schools, children laid the slates on their laps. Some brought rags or a sponge from home to clean the slates, but a favorite technique among boys was to spit on the slate, then wipe it off with a shirtsleeve. Parents or teachers made blackboards by coating a smooth board or a sheet of iron with black paint. Later, sheepskin erasers became available to wipe off the chalk.

Mothers made ink at home from pokeberry juice or by boiling the inner bark of a blackjack tree, then mixing the liquid with copperas, a green sulfate, to make it thicker. Or they boiled oak bark with a piece of iron. Some mothers made a fairly good ink

This drawing of a "badly arranged school room" appeared in an 1897 report on Missouri's public schools. It shows few teaching or learning materials. However, according to other reports, some schools had maps and, according to a Cooper County School superintendent, reporting in 1869, "few, if any, are without that indispensable article to the live teacher, the blackboard." (State Historical Society of Missouri, Columbia)

from mashing oak galls or "ink balls." Those were knotlike growths on trees filled with black spores. Store-bought ink could come in powder form to be mixed with water. Late in the 1800s, a popular ink was purple Carter's Ink. In winter, the ink often froze in the inkwells in the corner of the desktop and had to be thawed out before lessons.

The finest quill pen was made from a white goose feather. Other quills were made from turkey, swan, and crow feathers. The barrel or point of each feather was cut and shaped to form a nib. "Rules for Teachers in 1872" advised teachers, "Make your pens carefully. You may whittle nibs to the individual taste of the pupils." Students carrying pocket knives cut their own points. The first practical fountain pen was not available until 1884. Pencils with attached erasers changed the traditional usage of ink and pens in schools.

Spencerian Script was a popular handwriting technique used in schools. A strong connection was made between good penmanship

The teacher often prepared a quill pen for a student, but schoolboys carried pocketknives, called penknives, as a necessary part of their school supplies. Considerable evidence survives on old school desktops to show that some boys used their penknives to mark their place in the history of the school. (State Historical Society of Missouri, Columbia)

and good character (neatness indicated self-discipline). If a person was told he or she "wrote with a good hand, a nice hand" it was intended as a compliment. Spencer designed the oval shapes of his letters to match the water-smoothed pebbles he saw on beaches as a boy, and he worked in flowing curves to mimic the rhythmic sweep of waves. Learning to write was not easy for left-handed children. "I remember the second grade at Walnut Grove School in Clinton County," wrote Ruth Bowers of Plattsburg. "The teacher would smack my left hand each time I used it. She wanted me to use my right hand. Of course, it broke me of writing with my left hand." Many early scholars suffered this same experience.

Before paper tablets were available, children practiced their writing using "copy books" made from rags. The rags were cut, sometimes ruled, and then sewed together and bound with wax thread. Scholars wrote from one edge of a page to the other, careful to use every possible inch of space so that no cloth was wasted. The paper available was rough and unruled.

The books used by the earliest students were most often provided by the parents. These might include a copy of the Bible, a hymnal, the New Testament, *Kentucky Preceptor*, *The Tales of Peter Parley*, *Lessons in Elocution*, *Introduction to the National Reader* by John Pierpoint, an almanac, or a dictionary. Books were usually small and compact with fine print and dull colors. Teachers prepared their own textbooks when necessary.

In 1855 State Superintendent of Schools E. C. Davis recommended specific textbooks to accompany the curriculum. This marked the beginning of the twelve-year course of study required to graduate from Missouri's schools today, from kindergarten through high school. For the first time a systematic approach to learning was offered to teachers. When students moved from one common public school to another, they could continue learning from the same books and curriculum. Among those books chosen was the ever popular and often affectionately spoken of "blue-back speller." Lennis Broadfoot in *Pioneers of the Ozarks* describes a typical scene at Evening Shade School located in southeast Phelps County:

> Pioneer boys and girls of the hills . . . in tattered clothes and bare feet, carrying lunch baskets, slates, and blue-back spelling books, trekked over the winding mountain trails from all directions, leading up to the door to where they sat under the clapboard roof of this little ramshackle hut so cozily nestled under the low-swinging branches of the evergreen forest, to acquire what they termed, "the old blue-back speller education." By this they meant that the only book they had to study was the blue-back speller . . . while in conversation with the pioneer fathers and mothers, they are frequently heard to say, "Well, I hain't got nothin' only jist a blue-back speller education, 'cause pa and ma said that if we learned to read and write, that wuz good enough."

The "blue-back speller" was Noah Webster's *Standardized American Speller* with a blue binding. Spelling was learned by

The OLD BLUE-BACK SPELLER

was erstwhile thumbed by how many who read these words! And the old familiar picture! —e a c h heart recalls a different scene, but all remember well how, cribbed cabined and confined while sunshiny afternoons dragged their slow length along, the feeling akin to pity grew into real admiration for the "young sauce-box" who would NOT come down, either for words or grass.—It TAKES stones and bull-dogs to drive boys out of STARK Trees!

STARKTREES BEARFRUIT

The "blue-back speller" was so well known that Stark Brothers Nurseries and Orchards of Louisiana, Missouri, used it to draw attention to the superiority of its fruit trees. Finishing the blue-back speller was all of the schooling some children had. A former slave, Harry Johnson, interviewed in St. Louis reported, "I only went to school three days in my whole life, but a colored friend taught me how to spell out of a blue back spelling book . . . I can't write at all." (Stark Brothers Nurseries, courtesy of Madeline Matson)

syllables. The word *after* was learned by first reciting *af* (spoken as a syllable) then saying each letter—*a* then *f*. The next syllable was spoken, *ter,* and then each letter in that syllable, *t, e, r,* was spelled out. Finally, the whole word was pronounced, *after.* The speller was used in place of a reading textbook when none was available, and older editions contained "quaint" stories, information on the pronunciation and spelling of names, and long lists of abbreviations.

Often on Friday afternoon a spelling contest ended the week's work. Two students would be chosen as leaders. They would then "choose up" spellers for their teams, which lined up opposite each other. The teacher or another student "gave out" the words. If a student missed a word, he or she left the line. The spelling continued in this way until all but one student remained standing. That side claimed victory.

The blue-back speller led to enthusiastic spelling bees. Schools competed with each other. In *The History of Rural Schools of Putnam County*, one scholar describes such a competition:

> Dade Johnson was the teacher at the Hupp School, . . . where we went to a spelling bee. . . . After the match was finished, Mr. Carr challenged the school against we four brothers. I turned down seven, Jim floored ten, and John five or six and Sam had a bunch of the best spellers. After all were spelled down but one girl, Mr. Johnson pronounced the word "quire," meaning 24 sheets of paper. Sam said, "If you mean a body of singers I will spell 'choir'". "Next," said Dade Johnson, and the girl spelled "quire". Mr. Carr protested and the lights were blown out and the spelling bee broke up in disorder.

Spelldowns swept through the state as social entertainment. The *Louisiana Journal* on April 23, 1875, reported, "Warrensburg promises a grand spelling match for Johnson County to come off on the 20th of May. The best speller is to get forty acres of land for a prize."

More textbooks were available by the 1850s. A student might have a copy of Joseph Ray's *Rudiments of Arithmetic* or *Pike's Arithmetic*. These books started with simple addition and subtraction and progressed to square roots and complicated geometry. The object of this lesson from *Rudiments of Arithmetic* was to "combine practical utility with scientific accuracy":

> Question: The public lands are disposed of at $1.25 per acre: what will the government receive for a township containing 36 square miles?
> Answer: $28,800.

> Question: Letter postage is 2 cents for each ounce or fraction

thereof; what is the necessary postage on a letter weighing
1 and 1/4 oz?
Answer: 4 cents

Marmaduke Multiply's Merry Method offered rhyming arithmetic
lessons:

> 4 times 9 *are* 36
> Your medicine I will soon mix.
> . . . .
> 4 times 11 *are* 44
> Pray make this noise my dears no more.
> 4 times 12 *are* 48
> I hope that I shall get some Bait.

Ciphering (arithmetic) matches were popular both with students and with adults. The participants chose sides, and the side that answered first won a point. Some teams competed with other county schools for the county championship.

One of the most important studies during these early days was the study of geography. Scholars learned boundary lines, capitals, principal towns, mountains and rivers, regions and their natural resources. In one geography hunt activity, the students were divided into two teams. The teacher wrote the name of a river, town, country, or state on a blackboard or a piece of paper, and the side that found it first on the map won a point. Geography was so important to parents in Cedar County that an entire school building, Hazel Dell, was physically turned on its lot to face north using a mule, a windlass, and a cable. "The mule went round and round to wind the cable." The story handed down was that the "turn-about" was made to get the children facing north because, in geography class, they were taught that "up" was north. Since they sat with their backs to the door, their geography books and maps would then face the correct way.

From the attention given to the copying of maps and pictures, a new course entitled "drawing" was introduced in the public schools of Kansas City in 1869. This course was short-lived.

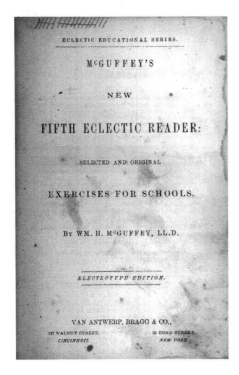

ECLECTIC EDUCATIONAL SERIES.

M^cGUFFEY'S

NEW

FIFTH ECLECTIC READER:

SELECTED AND ORIGINAL

EXERCISES FOR SCHOOLS.

By WM. H. M^cGUFFEY, LL.D.

ELECTROTYPE EDITION.

VAN ANTWERP, BRAGG & CO.,
137 WALNUT STREET,   28 BOND STREET,
CINCINNATI.   NEW YORK.

This is the title page in a McGuffey's Reader, copyrighted in 1857, owned by the author. Perhaps an early owner was counting the days until the end of school. (State Historical Society of Missouri, Columbia)

According to the first annual report of the superintendent of Kansas City's public schools, dated 1869–1870, some "regarded the study as involving a useless expenditure of money and a foolish waste of the children's time . . . and, as a natural consequence, they were extremely reluctant to furnish the required drawing books."

McGuffey's Readers were popular. First published in 1836, the books in the series taught honesty, industry, courage, and politeness. Passages from the Bible and Shakespeare and stories such as "Boy on the Burning Deck" and "Old Oaken Bucket" were included. William Holmes McGuffey, a teacher, compiled the eclectic readers. The stories and poems usually had a pious or patriotic theme. Students memorized much of the content and learned moral and character-building lessons from selections such as "Respect for the Sabbath" and "Control Your Temper."

Weald's Improved Reading Made Easy contained lessons consisting of words of one and two syllables, teaching good behavior with conclusions to stories such as: "A good child will do as he is bid," "Mark the child who does well, and do so, too," and "We must not do a bad deed: if we have done so once, we must do so no more." While reading, the pupil was required to "hold an erect posture, with chest thrust forward, so as to give as large a space as possible for inhaling atmosphere into the lungs."

Children and parents knew to take care of the few textbooks available so they could be passed on to a younger brother or sister or sold to a neighbor. The lower-right-hand corner of the pages of some schoolbooks often became badly soiled from a licked thumb or finger turning the page. Scholars were lectured about this bad habit and given strict instruction not to lick their fingers. Students attending Post Oak School in Osage County recall using this as a way to tattle on someone. They would raise their hands and say, "Teacher, you know what? . . . Tom licked his thumb!"

Some teachers preferred vocal teaching. Their schools were nicknamed "blab schools." Reading, spelling, and arithmetic facts were learned by rote, reciting out loud. With only one or two books in the school, students repeated their lessons over and over until they were memorized. This account by a scholar of a blab school is in *Wilson's History of Hickory County:*

> Everyone in school, talked, read and spelled aloud. No student was ever punished for making a noise. It was the more quiet ones, who were scolded because they were regarded as not being studious if they did not make a noise in "getting" their lessons. At the busiest time during school hours you could hear the children a quarter of a mile away, spelling and reading. Some big "leather-head" of a boy would try to spell louder, when "getting" his spelling lesson than anyone in school, and he was usually commended by the teacher as the most studious boy in school.

Blab schools were popular in frontier days because many early settlers could not read. Memorized work was repeated to others for their enjoyment and helped in educating them. Also, paper was scarce, so most work was performed orally. Reciting lessons from a book proved that the scholar knew it. When State Superintendent E. C. Davis insisted on abandoning this "loud studying," those who disagreed with him still believed that constant listening to others recite or reading aloud oneself helped everyone learn.

Songs sung at home and in school taught moral lessons. A popular folk ballad told of a young girl, Charlotte, who froze to death one cold winter's night while on the way to a party, because she wanted to "show off" her new dress and would not cover herself with a coat or blanket. There were many versions of the ballad. Charles Ingenthron of Walnut Shade, Missouri, sang the first four verses this way for collector Vance Randolph:

> Young Charlotte lived on a mountain side
> In a lone and dreary spot,
> There wasn't a house for five miles around
> Except her father's cot.
>
> In a village fifteen miles away
> There's a merry ball tonight,
> The air is cold and chill as death
> Her heart is merry and light.
>
> Oh daughter, oh daughter, the mother said,
> Those blankets round you fold
> For this is a dreadful night abroad
> You'll catch your death of cold.
>
> Oh nay, oh nay, the daughter said
> And she laughed like a Gyptian queen,
> For me to be wrapped up in blankets like this
> I never could be seen.

Miriam Lynch of Notch, Missouri, had an old manuscript book with "The Song Ballet of young Shallity." The last stanza read:

> Come all young girls and warning take
> Your parents be sure to obaye,

This photograph was part of an educational exhibit Missouri sent for the U.S. Centennial Celebration in Philadelphia in 1876. The Dozier School District was in an area in far west St. Louis County, roughly in the neighborhood of present day Allenton and Eureka. (Special Collections, St. Louis Public Library)

> Remember the faith [fate] of Young Shollity dear
> Who froze to death in the slay [sleigh].

In the mid-1800s, problems remained in establishing a statewide common public school system. Butler County, typical of so many other counties in Missouri, gave the following reasons for its slow progress in establishing schools:

(1) Lack of education among the early settlers
(2) The philosophy of education in the background of most of the early settlers
(3) Limitations in Missouri school laws
(4) Isolation of the settlements, and
(5) Lack of money

Chapter Eight

The Slow Progress of Common Schools

In this part of the country education has been neglected.
... As there is no school here, I have proposed to the children to instruct one another. This they do; each family thus becomes a little school.

— Charles Herbert of Parkville, Missouri, letter to
American Home Missionary Society, April 1, 1846

In 1840, less than 40 percent of those eligible attended public schools. W. B. Starke, the superintendent of common schools, reported during the years before the Civil War that more than one hundred thousand children in Missouri had no visible means of instruction. "The extreme apathy of the people in some neighborhoods and sections of the state is manifested by the utter absence of any effort in this great cause." He emphasized the importance of every person possessing "the intelligence and learning to guide . . . and the oral sense to control." Even as late as 1854, nine-tenths of the schools in the state were dismal, dreary one-room buildings standing by themselves in an open area.

It was not until eight years after Charles Herbert wrote the American Home Missionary Society about his plan for having each family become "a little school" that a Mr. McDonald opened the Parkville District school in the basement of a Methodist church in 1854. The farm home, the country church, and neighbors were still the most important influences in the

Throughout the nineteenth century, many children worked long hours on the farm, in factories, or in mines, leaving little time for schooling. By 1900 only 76 percent of children aged six through twelve were in public schools, and the laws still allowed employers to work children between the ages of fourteen and sixteen up to fifty-four hours per week, or six nine-hour days. The tiff mine shown here was approximately seven feet deep and four feet in diameter. (Photo courtesy of National Child Labor Committee, New York, State Historical Society of Missouri, Columbia)

education of Missourians. Although one out of every five Missourians was of school age, common schools claimed little attention from the state.

Those who supported the common school concept, and wanted legislation to provide for it, persisted and intensified their efforts. More unsettled land was claimed. Community leaders tried to develop schools in most towns and cities. Road maintenance improved, making schools more accessible to the growing numbers of students in rural areas. With all these changes and with continued effort, Jefferson's theory of education for all gradually moved forward for white children.

The most important influences on education, both good and bad, came from the legislature. In 1847, legislators passed a law prohibiting education for blacks whether slave or free. John Berry Meachum, who had worked with John Mason Peck in St. Louis in the 1820s, made attempts to educate black children in the basement of his church. Threatened with jail because the law prohibited his activities, he anchored one of the steamboats he owned in the middle of the Mississippi River, establishing a floating "Freedom School." Anchoring the boat on the river placed it under the authority of the federal government, rather than the state government. Meachum set the tuition at one dollar per month, ferrying the students by skiff to and from his floating school. Records show that hundreds of African American children were educated in this Freedom School on the river during the 1840s and 1850s, but by 1860, just prior to the Civil War, as few as 155 free black children attended a school.

The education act of 1853, intended for white children, provided the necessary state financing and more supervision of schools. Twenty-five percent of all the state revenue collected was appropriated for the state's schools. In 1858, $309,000 went toward funding schools. The county commissioners, now under state supervision, had the responsibility of examining teachers applying for a school position, deciding on a course of study, selecting textbooks, and inspecting every district school.

Moniteau County Commissioner J. M. Hardy's entries in his daily log show the diverse conditions of rural schools in 1860. On his visit to District 2, Township 43, Range 16, Hardy found the school to be "doing rather better than many others. Instruction more thorough. . . . Government [organization] as good as others. The teacher seems interested in his employment, and [wishes] to avail himself of all the help derived from books and maps." In District 4, Township 45, Range 17, the school had "good seats, but no library or maps. Teacher very well posted in our common textbooks, but rather deficient in energy and government." He noted that the teacher had "not chosen teaching as a profession and therefore does not feel interested in establishing a character as a teacher." Visiting District 2, Township 44, Range 17, he reported: "Found the school well conducted. Instruction thorough and government good. Female teacher—she has chosen teaching as a profession. The patrons have been notified and several of these were present to hear the lecture." In District 3, Township 44, Range 16, he visited "a bond school—the first I have visited of the kind, order and government very good. Recitations are almost impossible in vocal studying schools. Not much money in this district except what is raised by rate bill." A school in District 2, Township 46, Range 14, he found to be "a small badly arranged house and no evidence of thorough instruction—school about as good as none." In District 3, Township 45, Range 14, the school was "small from some cause. Spelling, reading, writing, arithmetic, grammar and geography are taught. . . . Order and government moderate, teacher paid from the school fund entirely. School house not good—poorly arranged and not furnished at all."

Hardy's reports from September to December 1860 described many poorly managed schools and instruction "not as good as it ought to be." He reported that "a number of persons may keep a school, but few really teach." Several schools taught only small children or infants. Only one school, out of the twelve he visited, taught singing and music. Hardy's most favorable comments were written about a school taught by the Reverend J. W. Johnson. It was "tolerably large, instruction thorough, order good, and the scholars somewhat advanced. On the whole the school is rather better than most of the schools."

Free schooling was still thought of by many as "charity" rather than a basic right. Claude Phillips in A History of Education in Missouri reports that one "school board received a most violent condemnation from many sources" when it tried to institute free education. A newspaper charged that the decision "would open the schools to the lowest classes of the community, who would take possession of them, and drive out the better classes and degrade the schools."

Those children fortunate enough to be in public schools met on a common level, all following the same rules and enjoying the same rights. Students throughout the state studied the same subjects and had the same opportunities. By the 1850s, teachers were required to teach fundamentals in the social virtues, and children were to learn self-control and self-discipline. Rather than the prior harsh discipline aimed at forcing children to learn, students were persuaded to take more responsibility for "being good." Heavy emphasis was placed on the idea of a self-governed student.

William A. Mowry, a professional teacher in rural schools for more than fifty years, suggested that "the country schools and teachers performed a unique socializing function." The farm, he explained, furnished only family members as companions. But the district school to a large extent remedied this defect and gave the best social stimulus to children. Here the boys received their first lessons in true democracy. "To all are accorded the same rights, to all are assigned the same tasks, in all the same powers are developed and all are subject to the same discipline. Each boy measures himself with his peers."

In A Century of Childhood, 1820–1920, the authors describe the textbooks available later in the century as portraying heroes and heroines, "patriots who were moral because they were honest, diligent and enterprising. They were public servants rather than ministers, political stewards rather than religious authorities, politicians rather than churchmen . . . the example of the good child to the example for the wayward, and the advantage of goodness over evil demonstrated." And women, who were often deprived of an education, were beginning to be thought of as the "proper guardians of the classroom."

An article written in the early 1860s by Benjamin W. Hall, a teacher in Hickory County, argues for more education for women but is expressed in the context of nineteenth-century beliefs about the place of women in the field of education.

> An erroneous opinion prevails to a considerable extent in the West that it is a matter of small consequence in every community whether the female part of society is educated or not. . . . Let us educate our little girls properly. . . . Mothers possess more influence over the minds of very young children than fathers do. The fondness of a mother's love—how strong it strikes the sense! . . . Admitting that

mothers are with little children three times as much as fathers, we shall have to admit that they make three-fourths of the early impressions that are made on the infant mind. Then I am in favor of giving school girls a thorough training in the rudiments of the mother tongue. . . . I am of the opinion that females may be profitably employed in learning perfectly the rudiments and elementary principles of the mother tongue in order that they may be able to teach it then perfectly to little children that will ultimately fall to their care. . . . If the scholastic population was so small as not to be worth the attention of a schoolmaster of any note, we might procure in many instances the service of some competent female. This is often the case where there are any found competent. The reason why it is rarely the case that any female in a neighborhood is found competent is because they are so miserably neglected. Were we generally to commence a regular common school system and resolve to employ none but competent instructors to take charge of our children at first and send our girls as well as boys, we would soon find the great work would go rapidly on. While boys might be pushed a little forward to the manly arts, we could find an abundant employment for our little girls in learning the rudiments perfectly well so that they might be prepared to teach little children and such as may fall under their care. In this manner, learning would rapidly spread. We should soon see the surprisingly wonderful effects thus produced on society.

In the late 1840s, a new wave of immigrants was arriving in Missouri from Germany, Ireland, Italy, Scotland, Sweden, Poland, Norway, Switzerland, Holland, Wales, and Yugoslavia, all speaking the languages of their homelands. Cultural differences created difficulties for teachers of the newly arrived children. Too often, teachers suppressed the children's cultural background, and their Old World customs of dance, music, and folklore were overlooked by teachers in their eagerness to instill a love for America.

The various English dialects spoken were sometimes a difficult barrier for teachers to overcome as well, as more and more

STAR SCHOOL HOUSE
Dist. No. 38, Barry County, Missouri
Donated by
Mr. and Mrs. Don Sater
- - - An extension of - - -
The Ralph Foster Museum
The School of the Ozarks

For the most part, rural areas of the state suspended educational efforts during the Civil War, but in 1863 two mothers in Barry County were determined that children should be able to go to school. With the help of neighbors, they built a log school about two miles from a Union encampment, and for four years the mothers taught the children. In 1867 state funds became available, and a new clapboard school was built. The first paid teacher was Captain George Stubblefield, who had seen action at Wilson's Creek. The school building is now part of the Ralph Foster Museum at the College of the Ozarks. (Drawing by Steve Miller, used by permission of Ron Miller, courtesy College of the Ozarks)

children from different regions arrived and attended school. "Although the English language changed rather rapidly in the 18th century few of these changes affected the American colonies English," wrote Ozark folklorist Vance Randolph. Mildred McCormack, a teacher at King's Point School north of Thayer, said, "The idea was for [students] to control the language, not let the language control them." She heard expressions such as "I be goin'," "It bain't right," and "He drag throo, thataway." As English, in its various dialects, began replacing French as the principal language, the *Missouri Gazette* in St. Louis carried only occasional notices in French. Educators such as Noah Webster continually encouraged the use of one common national language: "We ought not to think of ourselves as people of one state

. . . but as Americans." The concept of the United States as a "melting pot" developed soon after the American Revolution.

There were still places in Missouri where English was seldom spoken, although the state required it to be taught as the single language in most schools. In the Union community, southwest of Houston, Missouri, a teacher, Gary Koch, taught a half-day German-speaking school and a half-day English-speaking school. German was still the primary language spoken in Hermann, and French the language of Ste. Genevieve and the Old Mines Community of Washington County. It was not until the early twentieth century that children of French families in Old Mines were not allowed to speak French at school.

As the roles of teachers changed, the log cabin schoolhouse began a slow transition in some areas. Boards covered the dirt floor. A new patented wooden desk with iron-legged chairs attached replaced the puncheon bench. In the 1850s, W. B. Starke, superintendent of common schools, recommended a box-car-shaped frame school building. Sometimes a school even had a belfry with a dinner bell built on the roof and a porch gable added to shelter the entrance. Clocks, wall maps, alphabet cards, and globes were available. Coal- or wood-burning stoves replaced the open fireplaces. Some schools had the luxury of a well for water and of glass windows. A platform at one end of the room served for recitations and raised the teacher's desk.

But the slow progress in education virtually stopped as the Civil War began. As Selwyn Troen wrote in *The Public and the Schools:*

> The urgency of the moment was captured in the title of the bill that forced the closing of the schools: "An Act to Raise Money to Arm the State, Repeal Invasion, and Protect the Life and Property of the People of Missouri." Preparations for war necessarily took precedence over the education of children. Guns were more important than books.

During the war years (1861–1865) no state revenue was available for education. Male teachers left to fight for the Union or the Confederacy or went west. The few female teachers returned home to their families. Abandoned schoolhouses were destroyed by fires set by vandals or by travelers trying to keep warm in the only shelter available. Guerrilla raiders used some schools as stables or to hold supplies of food and ammunition. Some served as hospitals for the wounded.

One exception was the Star School. In the *White River Valley Historical Quarterly*, Bill Cameron described the history of "An All-American One Room School with a Proud name STAR":

> In a year of war 1863 in a lovely place in the Flat Creek Valley in Barry County, Missouri, near the junction of Willow Branch and Flat Creek two mothers saw the need for a school where children could be taught the essentials of education; reading, writing and arithmetic and be subjected to kind but effective discipline. . . . For four years those mothers taught the children without receiving any monetary reward.

Star School now stands on the campus of the College of the Ozarks in Point Lookout as a example of the one-room school.

Although St. Louis schools and others in larger Missouri towns did reopen after the war started, most schooling had to be postponed as battles between Union and Confederate sympathizers and deadly raids by guerrilla bands on both sides raged throughout the state. In most parts of Missouri the only safe place for a child was at home.

Chapter Nine

Rebuilding Missouri's School System "Without Regard to Color"

In consequence of the war, which has with unparalleled ferocity and bloodshed devastated our state for the last 20 months, the common schools of the state are prostrated and broken up. Schoolteachers have laid down the ferrule and taken up the sword; and parents have sent their children to learn war on the battle plains, instead of letters in quiet groves of literature and science.

— Mordecai Oliver, superintendent of common schools, reporting to the Twenty-second General Assembly

I n the years following the war, Missouri had a desperate need for both black and white teachers. Few African Americans had been trained or allowed to teach before the Civil War. During and after the war, white teachers had to take the "Iron-Clad Oath," a loyalty oath affirming their innocence of eighty-six different acts of disloyalty against Missouri or the Union. The oath listed such acts as giving aid or comfort to any hostile person; giving money, goods, letters, or information to the enemies of the United States; or harboring or aiding any person engaged in guerrilla warfare. Missourians who had committed any of the acts could not teach in any public or private school. Many whose sympathies were with the Confederacy had in one way or another engaged in these activities and still had strong feelings about their loyalties. The Iron Clad Oath eliminated many qualified teachers.

Officials developed the oath in different forms. The provost marshal's office in St. Louis recorded the oath of allegiance given by Sue M. Bryant of Cooper County to the assistant provost marshall in St. Louis:

> [I,] Sue M. Bryant of Cooper county, State of Missouri, do hereby solemnly swear that I will bear true allegiance to the United States and support and sustain the Constitution and laws thereof; . . . that I will discourage, discountenance and forever oppose secession, rebellion and the disintegration of the Federal union; that I disclaim and denounce all faith and fellowship with the so-called Confederate armies, and pledge my honor my property and my life to the sacred performance of this my solemn oath of allegiance to the Government of the United States of America.
> Subscribed and sworn to before me this 10th day of October, 1864 at St. Louis, Mo. Wm. A. Keyser, Asst. Prov. Mar.

During the war, some citizens had reported acts of disloyalty by teachers. In a typical testimony, subscribed to on July 31, 1863, a Miss Kate Boone gave a sworn statement about an acquaintance of hers. The document is now preserved in Missouri's Union Provost Marshal papers in the Missouri State Archives:

> I live in Danville and [am] well acquainted with Miss Susan Hughes who is teaching a school in Danville. I saw Miss Hughes on 29 inst—after she had been ordered to take the oath of allegiance and after she had taken the oath and filed it in the clerk's office—at Mr. Winters house in Danville—she said she had been up at Head Quarters but had not taken the oath. She cheered twice for Jeff Davis and the Southern Confederacy and said Price would be along after while. She said she had not taken the oath and would not take it, and that she would teach school too.

As schools opened again around the state, the majority of the teachers were men who had served in the Union Army. They had returned with a wide range of experiences, having traveled far from their local communities, and filled an immediate need. The first schools to open were crowded with young men and women who had had no opportunity to attend school during the war years, although some came for only one or two days to learn how to write their names.

These earliest schools were for whites, but some residents recognized the need to educate black children as well. Lafayette County preservationist Charles Sands found evidence that in the winter of 1865–1866 the congregation of the German Methodist church in Lexington opened a school for newly freed slaves in the community. An experienced teacher, Miss M. E. Parker, taught approximately seventy students in the basement classroom of the church, assisted by Elizabeth McFarland. The school continued in the church for two years.

Northern religious groups also worked to educate black children. Emma Ray, born a slave in Springfield in 1859, wrote of her early schooling by missionaries in her autobiography, *Twice Sold, Twice Ransomed*. Carla Waal and Barbara Korner published excerpts from her work in *Hardship and Hope*. Emma's mother had died in 1868, leaving nine children. In order to keep his family together, Emma's father let the children "work out" for local families.

> In the fall of the year, after working in the summer time, the children that were old enough were sent to school. Two of us girls were old enough; our three brothers and oldest sister had no chance to go; they had to work. Our white school-teachers, sent from the North, were devout Christians and missionaries. They taught us not only to read, but also to study the Bible and to learn the ways of God. . . . I did not go very steadily. I worked out in the summer and went to school in the winter. . . .
>
> Part of the time I did not have enough to eat. I have gone to school many a day without having anything to eat

until night, with the exception of a piece of cold corn bread. When I saw other girls, who had mothers, have good things to eat in their dinner pails, I would hide mine. I thought then as much of a white-flour biscuit as I would of the finest fruit-cake now. . . . I ofttimes took my little sister and went off by myself and ate my corn bread with sorghum molasses, if I was fortunate to have that, and I would never let them know but that I had dined sumptuously.

Emma went to school until she entered the fourth grade, often "with the sole of my shoe all loose and tied on with a string, through deep snows and zero weather." When the Christmas holidays came and "everyone was making presents for the Christmas tree in the church," she knew she and her little sister would have no presents, so she practiced her "first church deception." She and her sister wrapped wood chips in paper for one another. They could not open them in church, but they did have their names called when presents were distributed.

Emma's father wanted her to continue her education, but she preferred to work and buy clothes. She had learned to read and write and spell, which, as she wrote, "was considered among our people a pretty good education." She later married L. P. Ray and moved to Seattle, Washington, where she became the first president of the "colored" W.C.T.U. in Seattle.

As education once again became a top priority, delegates to the Missouri State Convention of 1865 drafted a new constitution, providing for the establishment and maintenance of free public schools for *all* persons in the state between the ages of five and twenty. Veterans past the age of twenty could return to school and attend free for a period equal to the length of time they had served in the Union Army. All funds were to be appropriated in proportion to the number of children without regard to color.

Even before the end of the war, Missouri had enacted an ordinance abolishing slavery, which declared, "hereafter in this state there shall neither be slavery nor involuntary servitude, except in punishment of crime, whereof the party shall have been duly

Black parents were eager to have their children learn, and some early teachers were amazed at the hardships parents endured to ensure that their children had the opportunity to learn to read and write. Once free, children learned both in school and from their neighbors. They also learned from white neighbors. Reportedly youngsters who lived near communities of German immigrants, such as Hermann, New Melle, Bethel, and Pleasant Grove, learned to speak their language, as their ancestors had learned French and English. (State Historical Society of Missouri, Columbia)

convicted, and all persons held to service or labor as slaves are hereby declared free." President Lincoln's Emancipation Proclamation, which took effect on January 1, 1863, had freed only those slaves in areas in rebellion against the United States. Since Missouri and other border states were not in rebellion, their slaves remained in bondage during the last years of the war. Missouri became the first state to free its slaves, celebrating Manumission Day on January 11, 1865, but most of the newly freed people faced starting from almost zero in terms of education as well as other skills needed in their daily lives.

Few opportunities to learn had existed for slaves or free blacks before and during the war. Most African Americans knew only what they had been able to learn from their association with one another or with the families of their former owners. Brought to the United States from different tribes in Africa, or separated from their tribesmen when they were sold, slaves had no common African language. They had learned the language of their owners. The first slaves in Missouri, brought to work in the lead mines, or for French missionaries, merchants, or fur traders, spoke French. Those brought by American settlers who came before or after the Louisiana Purchase spoke the English of their owners, and the dialects of the slaves preserved many old English terms they heard as they were sold from state to state. Many words often associated with "Black English"—*gwin* for "going," for instance, or *sebben* for "seven"—are actually archaic English forms, according to linguists. Many of the words in the stories and songs collected in the 1880s by Mary Alicia Owen of St. Joseph from black women in the community reflect the dialects to which black people had been exposed.

> Come, Lawd, come! Come ater me
> Ise looking todes sundown
> Come tek my han an set me free
> Ise looking todes sundown.

Speaking French or an English dialect made learning to read and write formal English difficult, but most teachers found that their black students were "generally" as quick as white students to learn. Joe M. Richardson quotes a teacher in St. Louis, who wrote, "the secret perhaps is their great anxiety to learn how to read." Their parents had learned how important it was to be able to read and write, and they wanted their children to have the same opportunities the white children did.

In districts with twenty or more resident black children, the state authorized separate schools for blacks, designating them "African schools." The law required a minimum of thirty white children or twenty black children in order for a school to be organized. If the attendance in any black school fell below twelve students in any month, that school closed for a maximum of six months and the students were, by law, if sometimes not actually, allowed to go to school with white students.

J. M. Greenwood, superintendent of the Kansas City public schools, called the school laws enacted in 1874 "a new chapter in the history of Missouri," adding that the enactments "met with violent opposition in many sections of the state. The conflict raged in town and country. In some localities the citizens positively refused to organize for school purposes." In Kansas City, he reported,

> There was not a public school building in the city. Disorganization reigned supreme. The city was utterly destitute of all school accommodations, and there was not a dollar for school expenses. The buildings that could be rented for school purposes were old deserted dwellings, unoccupied store rooms and damp, gloomy basements in some of the churches. . . . In October, 1867, the schools were formally opened in rented rooms, which had been hastily and scantily furnished. Into these unattractive abodes the children were huddled together to receive instruction.

Black leaders in St. Louis formed the Missouri Equal Rights League in 1865, appointing James Milton Turner as secretary. They circulated a petition throughout the state, urgently requesting the legislature to provide suitable schools for black children. The league also asked for an amendment to the Missouri Constitution to eliminate the word *white* to guarantee equality of the state's citizens. The following year the St. Joseph Board of Public Schools took action to eliminate the word *white* in all sections of its incorporation papers.

According to the Reverend Samuel A. Love, he became the teacher of the first Negro school in Liberty, in Clay County, in 1867 and in that same year he "was the first Negro commissioned by Governor Thomas Fletcher to do work in the State of Missouri for the establishment of Schools for Negro children."

In spite of the new laws, very few counties established schools for African Americans immediately after the Civil War, for several reasons. Many counties in the Ozarks did not have large numbers of slaves, and often they lacked the required twenty

Born to a slave mother on a farm near Diamond, Missouri, George Washington Carver attended school in Neosho. His scientific research on peanuts, sweet potatoes, and other food brought him national and international fame and helped improve economic conditions for southerners, both black and white. He attended the dedication of the school for African American children in Fulton named for him. (Photo by A. E. Schroeder)

students, as well as buildings and funds to pay teachers. In McDonald County in southwest Missouri, many school buildings had been destroyed, and the county had little money. A. M. Tatum, the school superintendent, reported that "five colored male and eight colored female children live in the county. There are 486 white male and 431 female children, six male teachers, two frame and nine log school buildings and $673.00 received from the state." With only thirteen black children living in the county, the state did not require a school for them.

Reports from Newton County were similar. Only a few school buildings remained: nine were log and two were frame. But there were 36 black male and 15 black female children in the county compared to 1,423 white male and 1,195 white female children. The law required Newton County to provide an "African school." George Washington Carver, born to a slave mother on the Newton County farm of Susan and Moses Carver about 1865, attended the school in Neosho in Newton County.

His career as a world-famous scientist had begun on the farm of his mother's owners, where Susan Carver taught him to read and write and he studied the plant life of the farm. The school in Neosho provided the next step in his education.

The Western Sanitary Commission in St. Louis organized classes for black soldiers at Benton Barracks. Mary A. Bell, whose father worked as a nurse at the barracks, told an interviewer collecting slave narratives that she went to classes with the soldiers for about six months. Bell, who was born in 1852, had been put out to work by her owner at age seven "to take care of three children" of a Presbyterian minister. At meal times "dey put me on a pony . . . to ride out to de fields and call the hands to dinner. After the meals . . . I helped in the kitchen, gathered the eggs, and kept plenty busy." After her six months of school at Benton Barracks, she attended school at St. Paul's Chapel and two other locations, altogether for about six years. She told the interviewer that she was "apt and learned fast."

Although some freed slaves stayed with their former owners after the Civil War, many left, some moving to St. Louis or Kansas City, some to other states. Between 1860 and 1880 the black population of St. Louis increased almost sixfold. Hiram Revels, a minister, had started a subscription school in 1856 that, according to historian William E. Parrish, was "the earliest known Negro-run school in St. Louis." Although Revels ran the school for only a year, he revived it during the war and worked with other teachers to establish a Negro board of education, which began operations in February 1864, taking over four subscription schools with a total of four hundred students. The Negro board of education did not charge fees, and in 1866 the St. Louis public education system took over the schools.

Many of the newcomers to Missouri were freed slaves from the southern states. Records for Kansas City and Springfield indicate that most blacks in those cities, as in St. Louis, came from the South. According to a Freedmen's Aid Commission Agent in Springfield, most "blacks locate in town because they are afraid to go into the country, but the life in town was not always safe." William E. Parrish quotes Sempronius H. Boyd's report:

> Hundreds of negroes from Arkansas have settled here
> [Springfield] and are industrious, well behaved and now
> constitute a large proportion of our laboring class and
> indeed is a great blessing to us. Yet I must say to you
> [General Granville M. Dodge] that they are cowered and
> frightened. They are persecuted & wronged, whipped and
> even killed and nothing done to prevent it or to hinder [it].

Parrish adds that black children were stoned as they made their
way to classes.

Thomas A. Parker, superintendent of schools, wrote in his
annual report for 1869 that there was a "desperate need for
negro teachers." Prejudice existed among both whites and
blacks when a white teacher taught in an African school.
Occasionally, a white person would threaten or attack another
white person teaching in a school for black children, so it was
difficult to find teachers. Few blacks had qualified for certification as teachers, and they often felt suspicious toward sometimes
patronizing and ill-trained white teachers. Both blacks and
whites resented the self-righteous attitudes sometimes shown by
white teachers sent by the American Missionary Association.

Poor pay was also a problem for those teaching in the African
American schools. As late as 1873, male teachers in a school for
black children received $46.70 a month, compared to the
$82.42 paid male teachers in a school for white children, possi-
bly because there were fewer children in the black school. In
cities where there were no schools for African Americans, black
and white ministers, teachers, or missionaries often offered
classes for a small fee.

As soon as education for blacks was made legal after the war,
Hiram Young, a free black man in Independence, Missouri,
worked to set up classes for blacks. As a wagon maker who had
earned enough to buy his freedom, he had become one of the
wealthiest men in Jackson County before the Civil War. As historian Antonio Holland wrote of Missouri's African Americans,
"some proved they could not only survive, but also achieve great
material success." The first classes organized by Young were

taught in the Second Baptist and St. Paul AME church. Two former slaves, Thomas Hale and William Tadlock, who had learned the rudiments of reading and writing, were the teachers. After the Independence Board of Education was established, a small room was rented from the German Methodist church for eight dollars a month to teach the "colored" children. Through Young's persistence and effort, a new school building was built in 1874 with eight rooms, one for each grade. The school was originally named Douglass, after Frederick Douglass, who escaped to freedom from Baltimore in 1838 and became a renowned abolitionist, writer, and orator. It educated each student for only two years. That was all the white community believed that black students needed. Douglass School was renamed Hiram Young School in 1934.

Some county school superintendents who did not have enough black students for a separate school sent those students to white schools when no objections were raised. Other counties managed to establish schools for black children. Iron County in southeast Missouri reported a total of twelve schools—seven primary schools, one high school, one seminary, two select schools, and one school for "colored pupils." Since few schools for black children had been established by 1868, the legislature lowered the number of eligible children required to start a school from twenty to fifteen.

James Milton Turner, by this time an agent of the Freedman's Bureau, was appointed by the Missouri Department of Education in 1869 to travel throughout the state advising counties on building schools where there were enough eligible students and reporting on the condition of black schools already in existence. During the next four years, Turner traveled ten thousand miles examining schools, often finding the few schools designated for black students in a rundown condition. Turner, who taught in the first school for African American children in both Kansas City and Boonville, was an important leader in raising standards and bringing education to black students.

A school that was to have a major positive influence on African American education in Missouri had its beginning

Concerned Citizens for the Black Community of Boonville worked to recognize the founder of Boonville's first African American School with this bronze statue of James Milton Turner in the city's Morgan Street Park. Born in slavery, Turner attended Oberlin College and served in the Civil War. He was wounded at the battle of Shiloh. After the war, he returned to Missouri to work for educational opportunities for African Americans and moved to Boonville in 1869. (Photo by Richard Schroeder)

when soldiers in the Sixty-second and Sixty-fifth United States Colored Infantry, stationed in Texas, began to dream of a school in Missouri that could educate black people. With contributions from the officers and from their own pay, they managed to raise more than $6,000.00. The soldiers persuaded one of their officers, Richard Baxter Foster, a native of New Hampshire, to help them with their dream. After Foster received his discharge, he went first to St. Louis to try to carry out his promise, but was unable to get a school started there. He moved to Jefferson City, where he finally got permission to use an old abandoned school on Hobo Hill. "What a sanctuary!" he wrote. "The rains pour through the roof scarcely less than outside. I could throw a dog through the side in twenty places. There is no sign of a window, bench, desk, chair, or table." The school opened in September 1866 with two students and Foster as the teacher. Before long it was so crowded that he needed an assistant. Dr. G. B. Winston, a member of the board of education, pointed out in his report, "In the colored school (Hobo Hill) there was not a thermometer

John Jeffreys of Columbia was eighteen when he went to Jefferson City to enlist in the Union Army. Assigned to the Sixty-second United States Colored Infantry, he served in Texas and was among those who raised funds to build a school in Missouri to train black teachers. Lincoln Institute, now Lincoln University, opened with two students on September 17, 1866. (Lincoln collection, Inman E. Page Library, Lincoln University, Jefferson City)

to indicate temperature, no stove or fuel; the glass in many of the windows was broken and the room was uncomfortably cold. The children were indifferently and thinly dressed and measles spread among the pupils."

In *The Soldier's Dream Continued: A Pictorial History of Lincoln University of Missouri*, Antonio F. Holland reported that by 1871, with the help of Howard Barnes, a local black businessman, Lincoln Institute was able to "erect on the site of today's campus its first building." In 1879, the state provided support to establish Lincoln Institute as a normal school for training black teachers. Foster had fulfilled his promise to the black soldiers. As its officials note, Lincoln University today provides "educational opportunities for a diverse student population in the context of an open enrollment institution. Its programs are grounded in the arts and sciences and focused on preparing both black and white students in public service professions. The school the black soldiers dreamed of has weathered many difficulties to fill a unique purpose in higher education in Missouri today."

But by 1870, only 21 percent of the black children in Missouri were attending schools, compared to 59 percent of the white children. Thirty-nine county superintendents reported that they did not have a school for blacks because they did not have the number of students required to establish one. In 1872 Wright County Superintendent J. T. Pope reported that the state superintendent of schools found that the problems still remaining were disadvantages peculiar to country schools and widespread throughout the state. Vearl Rowe, in *Sketches of Wright County,* lists these as "a widely scattered population, low taxable valuation on account of the large extent of unimproved property . . . short school terms, poorly qualified teachers, great variety of scholastic attainment, poor classification and impossibility of grading, frequent changes of teachers, and a labyrinth of text books." Finally, the state legislature allowed counties to establish schools by combining two or more districts to qualify. But often the result was that black students had a long way to travel to school, making regular attendance difficult.

In 1875, the St. Louis Board of Education established a black high school that included a normal department to train black teachers. Other areas showed progress as well. *History of Jasper County* reported that "W. R. McLane, a negro, was granted a teacher's certificate, August 23, 1877; was the first colored person in the county to successfully pass the examination, and was therefore the first colored teacher in the county."

Educational opportunities gradually improved as black teachers formed state teachers' associations. Black parents also kept active in their communities. The minutes from a school board meeting held in March 1880 in Canton show that a petition from the colored citizens of that community asked for a better school building to accommodate their children. During this time, Franklin School in Clay County taught seventy-three white children and six black children. California, Missouri, taught nine black students in a white school.

Improvements gradually came to African American schools as more black teachers were certified. A letter sent to the state superintendent by William J. Shaw, the Jackson County superintendent for Kansas City, shows that attitudes and conditions were changing slowly, but progress was being made.

In the matter of the education of the colored people, there are prejudices to overcome, and such influences have been brought to bear upon it as made it difficult, for some time, to obtain a person with sufficient nerve to undertake the duty of instruction in this city. It has, however, been accomplished, and a fine school is in operation. I know of no place in the county where they are of sufficient numbers to make school privilege practicable.

Well into the twentieth century, black schools were not controlled by the students' parents, but by members of the white community, who often made decisions for the school without input from black parents. An article in *Gateway Heritage* quotes a former student who recalled how some black parents in Callaway County adapted to the situation:

All of the school board members I guess during . . . the lifetime of that whole school were all white. Since the white community controlled the school boards, black citizens found other ways to be involved in the situations arising at school. Often this took place at work. Some of the parents of black students worked for [school] board members, in which case they discussed school affairs with their employers. This provided an information network which worked for both parties. Such was the case at Annabelle Taylor Branham's school. "My father worked for the president of our little district's school board. . . . So he had quite a bit of input. . . . Whenever anything went wrong . . . at the school, like the school was leaking or whatever, my father would go and tell them. Consequently we'd get it fixed right away."

In some cases, concerned white citizens established schools for black students. According to Marion Terrell Shaw, her grandfather Edward Davis Terrell built a school on his property in Saline County outside Marshall for black children. He and his wife were both teachers and knew the value of an education. The mother of several black students at the school did laundry for the Terrells and lived as a tenant on the farm, known as Trigg Place.

In some of the all-black towns that developed in Missouri after the war, residents established schools. A notable example was Thornlea School in Pennytown, also in Saline County. In their study, "Pennytown: A Freedman's Hamlet," Gary Kremer and Lynn Morrow report that Dr. Tom Hall of Arrow Rock assisted the Pennytowners with medical services and contributions. The school remained open until the early 1940s.

Penn School was founded in 1868 by Mrs. Sam Ellis, a white philanthropist, in the Westport area of Kansas City to educate the children of emancipated slaves. She rented a building on Penn Street. By the 1920s, a tiny school was established with two classrooms and two teachers. An unusually high number of graduates went into professional fields.

From 1875 to 1900, the Missouri public school system grew rapidly. Private schools, academies, and seminaries were often assimilated into the public system. Money for public schools was once again increased, this time to one-third of all general revenue. However, failure to comply with state laws and the lack of educated former slaves deprived blacks of schools in sparsely populated rural areas. Nonetheless, Missouri had established a black education system with primary schools in most areas.

As the century ended, the condition of both white and black rural schoolhouses and the quality of the education they were providing continued to be a major concern. Rural schools needed to be rebuilt and repaired. Education on every level in the state was reexamined and revised. White apathy, a lack of interest and concern, still undermined public schools for African Americans into the twentieth century.

Black communities persisted, however, in working to obtain schools for their children, giving the schools names that reflected African American history and achievement. The most popular names were Lincoln for President Abraham Lincoln and Douglass for Frederick Douglass. Attucks School in Bonne Terre in St. Francois County honored Crispus Attucks, the black Bostonian who led townsmen in a clash with British troops on March 5, 1770, losing his life in what became known as the Boston Massacre. Benjamin Banneker School in Parkville honors a freed man who helped survey and design the nation's capital. Educators Booker T. Washington and George Washington Carver and poet Paul Laurence Dunbar were often honored by having schools named for them. Schools in Kansas City and St. Louis were named for Senator Charles Sumner of Massachusetts, who opposed slavery before the war and after the war helped push through three amendments to the Constitution: the thirteenth, which abolished slavery; the fourteenth, providing equal protection under the laws for blacks; and the fifteenth, which granted black men the right to vote. Sometimes, though, the school for black children was simply given the same name as the school for white children, but with the designation *Colored*. In Boone County, Grindstone School was for white children, while Grindstone Colored School was for black children.

Today, many black citizens are working to preserve the historic schools that they and their children attended. Students at Union Chapel Elementary School in Parkville collected one million pennies ($10,000) in three years. In 2002, they donated that amount to help in the restoration efforts of the first African American school in Platte County—Banneker School, built in 1885. Field trips to historic black schools not only help Missouri's children learn about their state's history but also remind them of how far we have come from the segregated schools of the past.

Chapter Ten

A Gathering Place

One of the greatest events of the community in the winter
was the ciphering match. Everybody would come on horseback or in wagons, and bring their barn lanterns. We would
keep our feet warm to and from school with the lantern
and then use it to light the school building.
— Cynthia Lodge Hensen, who attended
Warren's Branch School outside Joplin

By the last decades of the nineteenth century, small-town
and rural schools had become social centers for both black
and white families in communities throughout the state.
The door to the schoolhouse was open for many community
events. The location was usually convenient for neighboring
families, and people of all ages, from all economic circumstances, came together to combat loneliness and isolation. They
laughed, prayed, listened to political speeches, debated current
issues, and gathered for sorrowful eulogies for a dead president,
a family member, or a community leader.

Families in rural areas or small towns often used the schoolhouse as a place to worship until a local church could be built.
Worshippers came for Sunday morning or Sunday evening services and Wednesday night prayer meetings. The denomination
of the service did not matter to most. The minister might be
Congregational, Presbyterian, Baptist, Methodist, or of another

faith. Church youth groups sometimes organized and met at the school for their monthly activities.

If a church was not soon built, funerals and memorial services were performed in the schoolhouse, which was sometimes next to a cemetery. Kenzie School, a log subscription schoolhouse in Butler County, was situated near the Kenzie Cemetery. Oak Grove School in Stone County was built in 1857 near the graves of a family named McCullah. A teacher at the school, T. C. Mitchell, taught a Sunday school class in the summertime under a large oak tree nearby and expressed a desire to be buried on that spot. At his death, his wish was granted. The cemetery is one of the oldest in the Ozarks. Prairie Church School in Lafayette County was on land owned by Colonel James Young. He gave 4.6 acres for the school and nearby cemetery. At Anders School 62 in Putnam County, Anders Cemetery joins the school grounds on the east. A cemetery known as God's Acre is located near Mt. Gilead School in Clay County. Benjamin Franklin Soper, the first teacher and a founder of the school, is buried in this cemetery along with members of his family.

Literary societies formed and met at the schools to read and discuss current books. Records show that "a very successful literary society was organized at Prairie View Schoolhouse, five miles southwest of Buffalo, Missouri. B. F. Johnson was appointed President and Mrs. Lena Sargent, secretary. The society meets on Friday night of each week." Some schools, as a way to make money to purchase textbooks, offered residents the opportunity to check out library books for a yearly fee. Franklin School, a subscription school that opened in 1847 in Clay County, limited circulation of the school's library books to "within eight miles," but strangers not known to the librarian in charge could not borrow books.

Communities commonly held orations and public debates at schools. Their motto was "to pursue the truth." On any occasion, a person might stand in front of the assembled group and give views on topics relating to religion, politics, education, or local concerns. Farming activities and seasonal chores determined when meetings or events would take place. The popular

One-room schools were still in existence in the mid-twentieth century. In 1941–1942 Betty Cook Rottmann of Columbia taught at this school in Gore, in Warren County, staying with a student's family and walking to school each day. (Courtesy of Betty Cook Rottmann)

months were from October to May. In 1889, the Dallas County Historical Society reported that "Peppers School was the scene for a joint discussion last night. The question was, 'Resolved, that the times indicate a downfall of the government.' The affirmative side gained the question. The negative side took a change of venue to Lone Rock School where the same question will be debated." Other popular topics were "Which is more important? Love or money? Fire or Water?"; "Is a woman's love stronger than a man's?" "Who did the most good for the Country . . . Washington or Lincoln?"

Following the Civil War, former slaves established churches where they could gather to worship and celebrate their freedom. These first churches often opened their doors for the education of both adults and children and became the center of the black community, sponsoring festivals, protest meetings, and conventions as well as providing schooling.

A small community on the southern edge of Liberty, Missouri, was settled by a group of freed blacks on land given to them by former slave owners. They built Mt. Olive chapel in 1912. This was later renamed White Oak Church, and a school built nearby was named White Oak School. The *Liberty Sun* reported on October 26, 1983, "It became a center of social and religious activities for the Negro people, and they built their homes around the church and a school. The teachers were not well trained, but they were anxious that the children learn basic abilities so they could take their place in the world." Behind the school is a cemetery on the bank of a creek. The family members of the church were baptized in the little creek that ran behind the school.

Well into the 1900s, children in Missouri attended one-room schools and teachers boarded with parents. Betty Cook Rottmann taught in Gore School in Warren County in 1941–1942 and recalls making her way on foot through the hills above the Missouri River to the schoolhouse, located on a little stream. As she wrote in *Memories and Memoirs:*

> As Betty [Cullom] and I first set out for school, Ace [Cullom] guided us—down the lane crossing their creek on a split log to the barn, up hills and down others, through gates and gaps, then across a neighbor's pasture, down his lane to the road, and at last across a low water bridge to school. I learned that a gap can be a twisted length of fence that must be unfastened from a post, and after one squeezes through, must be refastened by its wire loop, and woe to anyone who doesn't fasten it well. A low water bridge, I learned, isn't a bridge at all, usually just a concentration of gravel, in some places with the benefit of a bit of concrete, which one can cross if the creek is low. . . . After the first

rain, I asked Frances for her catalog and mailed my first order—a pair of knee-high pull-on rubber boots. From the day they arrived, I wore them.

Before the days of school custodians, parents in both black and white communities gathered for a combined work day and social gathering to repair and clean the school for the upcoming school year. They scrubbed and oiled wood floors, washed desks, polished and cleaned the pot-shaped stove and its flue, cut back grass surrounding the building, and repaired and painted the building itself. They brought basket dinners. Sometimes, the word was passed to families participating in the cleanup that each should bring a cake. A "taster" was chosen to be the judge and decide which cake was the best. Cooks who lost were sometimes disappointed in the decision and determined to bake the winning cake the next time. Parents' involvement resulted in students who took pride in their school, as is true today.

In many schools, a wintertime taffy pull was popular. Molasses (sorghum), vinegar, sugar, salt, and butter were all the ingredients needed. A fire was started and the ingredients mixed in a pot. When the taffy had boiled to the right consistency, it was cooled until it could be handled. Ben Land and his family in West Dent County, Missouri, had their own "taffy pullin'" technique, as described in *Pioneers of the Ozarks* by Lennis Broadfoot:

> The "kids" all gather in and take molasses and cook it down to a stiff candy called "taffy." Two "kids" will get out on the floor with one piece of taffy, and each will take an end of the piece in their teeth an' pull an' stretch an' eat it until it is all gone. The idea is to see who can eat the fastest and get the most candy. It's the durndest lot of fun you ever see'd.

Others might pull by choosing a partner, greasing their hands, and grabbing the taffy with their fingertips. The taffy was pulled to a length of about eighteen inches and then folded back, over and over. It changed from dark brown to a golden color after being pulled and twisted. It was a challenge to see who could pull the longest strand without breaking it. When it was stiff, the taffy was ready to eat. If it had snowed and someone had put runners on a wagon, the evening might include going for a sleigh ride, singing, and returning to school for treats of popcorn, apples, and taffy.

Box suppers, pie suppers, and candy suppers were held as fund-raisers for school supplies or books for the library. In hard times, there were even corn meal mush socials. For box suppers, ladies or girls sometimes painted and decorated their boxes with ribbons and flowers or whatever material was available. A supper for two was then packed in the box. Favorites were biscuits and jelly, sweet or white baked potatoes, or a chicken or meat sandwich made from chunks of beef or pork between chunks of thickly buttered bread. Pie supper boxes had anything from a piece of mincemeat pie to a slice of cherry pie, and candy supper boxes might be filled with taffy or homemade divinity fudge.

The boxes were numbered so that supposedly no one knew who had prepared which one, and then they were sold to the highest bidder. The successful bidder ate supper with the person who brought the box. Sometimes a young lady secretly told her "fella" which box was hers so they could eat together. A young man might bid his horse or a saddle or even a hog in the heat of the auction.

Another event was a basket supper followed by a "penny a vote" contest. Nominations were made for "the biggest baby," the most "love sick couple," and the "slowest person." As many votes could be cast by a bidder as he or she could afford pennies for each contest. And there were prizes for the winners. Booties might be given to the fellow with "the biggest feet." A mirror was the prize for the "ugliest man" or "prettiest girl." The most "henpecked husband" probably received a bantam hen. A prize for the "stinkiest feet" was given after those nominated removed their shoes and socks. That winner took home a bar of soap. A toy horn was the prize for the "windiest man." And the "sweetest girl" might take home a pound of sugar. The winners laughed, blushed, and occasionally got mad or cried, all of which added to the enjoyment of the others.

Drill teams were popular, and folk dancing, an impromptu play, or a speaker or musician could form part of the evening's entertainment at a fund-raiser. A square dance was popular for both adults and children. On occasion, the dances were held at the schoolhouse. With fiddlers in the background, the caller chanted directions to the dancers in time to the music. In preparation, the stove and all the benches or desks were moved from the center of the room and the floor was waxed. Women dressed up in their good Sunday clothes and men in their best overalls. Clapping, stomping, and jumping went on in the schoolhouse until long after midnight. Those familiar with square dancing will recognize "cowboy loop" and "sally good'in" and "roll the ball." Some churches banned dancing, and devout church members could not attend, but "play-parties" were sometimes held instead in communities where residents did not approve of dancing.

Family members took part in school Christmas programs, playing a shepherd, reciting a Christmas story, or singing Christmas songs. The students practiced for weeks. A nativity scene was the usual theme. One family would volunteer to cut a fresh evergreen tree to set up for the party. Weeks before the event, children were busy making decorations. They cut out paper snowflakes and pasted strips of colorful paper together, making red-and-green chains. Dried apple slices, popcorn, and berries were strung on the Christmas tree, which was lit with candles. Handmade invitations were carried home to parents announcing the Christmas event. Santa Claus or a school board member would arrive with gifts and candy for students. Children sometimes recognized Santa Claus. Melvin Goetz in Van Meter School recognized his father because of his scarred hand. At Sandhill School in Cedar County, Anna Lee Lower recognized her father from his shoes.

Schools might be segregated, but sometimes officials in schools for African American children invited their white friends to participate in special programs. In May of 1912 Douglass School in Columbia announced that the graduating address for the fourteen graduates would be made by Mrs. Luella St. Clair-Moss, the president of Christian College, adding that a section of seats had been reserved for "the white people who are cordially invited to attend the exercises. A small admission fee will be charged." In an article in the *Columbia Daily Tribune*, Sue Gerard of Columbia described visiting Grindstone Colored School with her children:

> They admired the handmade decorations on the windows and walls without comment. Mrs. Coleman came to greet us while her pupils stowed their books and papers inside their desks. She explained that the program that followed was entirely the work of the children.
>
> All eight grades had a part in it. Costumes appeared out of paper sacks, and the room was suddenly a stage with a live nativity scene. Angels sang on high; cattle and sheep made their usual noises. A lighted nativity creche sat in a cardboard-box stable. The characters were made of rolled-up newspapers, dressed and painted. Several soloists took turns kneeling before the creche, singing in high soprano voices as the other children chanted the familiar carols. . . . [Then] the pupils changed robes and shepherd's crooks to garb for the jingle-bells kind of Christmas.

A student at Cave Spring School District 47, in the southern part of Pulaski County, remembering programs planned on holidays, reported in *Pulaski County Rural Schools:*

> At Christmas and other times, like Halloween and Easter, the front of the room would be sectioned off with a wire and sheets. Then we would have a stage setting for our program. Everyone would memorize a poem or sing a song or have a skit of some kind. We even had our own school band. We made our instruments from can lids, with wooden spool handles, banged together. We had painted wooden sticks, cracked together, horseshoes hung by a string and hit with a nail, a piece of thin paper wrapped over a comb and blown on with your mouth, and even a couple of spoons beat together to help keep the rhythm. I was made the leader of the band! . . . I don't remember how we sounded, but how

can you hit a sour note or be sharp or flat with instruments like that. It sure was a lot of fun.

An annual photograph was taken at most schools. Photographs were expensive, and photographers were rarely available in rural areas, so parents took the opportunity to send all the children in the family to school for "picture day." Girls from the same family can often be recognized because their dresses were cut from the same bolt of cloth. Girls wore big bows in their hair, and boys might have a haircut for this once-a-year event. Many of the children seen in these photographs are barefoot, not necessarily from a lack of shoes, but rather because the photographer came in late spring when they had started going barefoot.

The last day of school was an exciting event. It was a time to invite parents, family and friends, the county supervisor, school board members, and all those interested in the community to participate. The schoolhouse was filled with bouquets of wildflowers, and children and visitors wore their best clothes for the event. Awards for "headmarks" in spelling, history, geography, and mathematics were presented. There were recitations, called "saying speeches," and the students proudly demonstrated their musical talent for parents.

Recitations included some as serious as "Brutus on the killing of Julius Caesar" or "Hamlet's soliloquy," others as lighthearted as "The Little Boy's Lament":

> Oh! why must I always be washed so clean
> And scrubbed and drenched for Sunday,
> When you know very well, for you've always seen
> That I'm dirty again on Monday?
> My hair is filled with the lathery soap,
> Which adown my ears is dripping;
> And my smartin' eyes I can scarcely ope,
> And my lips the suds are sipping.
> You rub as hard as ever you can,
> And you hands are hard, to my sorrow;
> No woman shall wash me when I'm a man,
> And I wish I was one tomorrow.

The mural of rural schools in the cafeteria of Maries R-1 School in Vienna was painted by John Viessman to show the progress of school buildings from the earliest log cabins to modern schools. (Western Historical Manuscript Collection, University of Missouri–Columbia)

The eighth-grade graduation ceremony was the biggest event of the day for those who had passed their written or oral examinations. The tests for eighth-grade graduation were prepared by the county supervisor and school board members. Some students were required to travel to the county seat prior to the last day's event and take a test given by the county superintendent of schools. The tests covered mathematics, grammar, and drawing maps by memory for geography. The students learned that day whether they had passed or failed. Those students who did not pass the first time could study and review and return for a second try at a later date. Sometimes students took oral tests on the last day of school in the presence of those attending the event. A few students who loved coming to school got permission to return the next year and repeat eighth grade even though they had graduated.

Autograph albums called "Remember Me" books were popular in the late 1800s and early 1900s. Students took them on the last day of school to have them signed by their classmates. Minnie Kapell in Morrison, Missouri, had these verses written in her book in 1894:

> Remember me early
> Remember me late
> Remember me dear Minnie
> And meet me at the gate [the gates of Heaven]
>   Your friend, Ida Estman

Minnie's brother had not mastered spelling, as seen in this verse:

> My pen is poor
> My ink is pail [pale].
> My love for you will never fail.
> Your brother, Fritz Kapell

Events at the school continued throughout the year. For black children an important occasion during the summer was Emancipation Day, traditionally celebrated on August 4. Fielding Draffen, who grew up in Saline County, wrote: "When I was a kid, August the 4th was sacred to black people. . . . By the threat of death you didn't even go to work on that day. You celebrated on that day. . . . It was considered a day you kind of reflected on what your ancestors came through and just kind of enjoyed the day."

A favorite summer activity in many communities was singing school. This was held after the crops were planted and lasted from one to three weeks. Anyone could sign up. A music teacher was employed as leader or director. Schools with pianos were favored, but the piano wasn't necessary. Sometimes an instrument accompanied the singers; however, all that was really needed was a tuning fork to give correct pitch so the class could sing a cappella. The director divided the group into a four-part harmony—sopranos, altos, tenors, and bass—using a scale of notes, *do, re, mi, fa, so, la, ti, do*.

In *History of a Missouri Farm Family: The O. V. Slaughters, 1700–1944*, the author wrote about an early singing school directed by his grandfather, Elijah Slaughter:

> Grandpa had at least three assets to qualify him as a teacher in a singing school. First, he had a tuning fork, and

you couldn't run a singing school of the old style without a tuning fork. . . . Second, Grandpa also had a very agreeable tenor voice. Not a big voice but a pleasant and a good voice. Third, he had a good ear. He knew when he was on pitch and he knew when someone else was on pitch. Also, off pitch. . . . Another piece of equipment that Grandpa must have had was a song book. . . . The do, re, mies were the foundation of the singing school. . . . So, Grandpa would stand up in front of his pupils. . . . He would hold up his tuning fork and strike it with a stick . . . or with something handy, to get the pupils started off on the right pitch. He would then run them through the do, re, mies, up and down, three or four times to limber them up and give them confidence, then they would turn to the music, a church song book. . . . And without a piano or an organ . . . all learned by sight and knowing the right pitch to give each do, re, mi. It was a miracle.

In some areas, an informal community meeting was held one evening a month at the schoolhouse, combining local business with socializing. Those who attended brought their needlework, exchanged recipes, and talked about the latest plow or that new contraption called an automobile or a cattle drive going through the county. They played cards or games of checkers or dominoes and challenged each other with riddles. They might even show off by reciting the names of the books of the Bible in order. If someone played the harmonica or knew a few songs on the accordion, music would enliven the event. And those present caught up on all the local news, made decisions on passing the school bond, and heard who might be "down on their luck" in the community. And, of course, many a tall fishing and hunting tale was told.

Through all these activities and meetings and sociables in small-town and rural schoolhouses, the "newcomers" and "old settlers" learned to understand and accept the "strange ways" of their neighbors. They learned about each other's customs, cultures, and beliefs. They found out about the many things they had in common. They learned to interact with all ages. They sang each other's songs. They danced one another's dances. Newly arrived immigrants learned to speak English through these associations in the schoolhouse as well as when to plow and plant. These socials contributed to individual self-esteem, helping some to overcome shyness and showing others it was all right to make a mistake. A closeness developed. The families learned to care about each other and share life's events in their one-room country school. It is no wonder, then, that so many called the school their second home.

In 1945, the editor of *Rural Education and Rural Life in Missouri* wrote in praise of Missouri's early schools:

> Missouri owes a great debt to her rural schools. A debt that can never be paid. Originating as a pioneer institution, the rural school was well-adapted to the needs of the times. It molded the lives of untold numbers of sterling men and women who have made the state strong. Admirably fitted to the open country of a free nation the rural school has been largely responsible for the success of our democratic ideals. In this, Missouri shares with the whole nation. Without the far reaching influence of this rural institution in the stabilization of our rural civilization there is a grave question whether our democratic form of government would have survived.

For More Reading

Education in Missouri: An Informal History (Jefferson City: Missouri Department of Education and Secondary Education, 1976).

The Genesis of Missouri: From Wilderness Outpost to Statehood, by William E. Foley (Columbia: University of Missouri Press, 1989), provides accounts of Missouri's colonial and territorial periods and explores the historical legacy of the state's diverse cultures—Indian, French, African, Spanish, and Anglo-American.

A History of Education in Missouri, by Claude Anderson Phillips (Jefferson City: Hugh Stephens Printing Co., 1911).

History of Education in Missouri, Autobiographical, by William Thomas Carrington (n.p., 1931), is a privately published study of schools and schooling in Missouri. Carrington discusses his experiences as a teacher in a one-room school and as state superintendent of public schools from 1899 to 1907. "I favored standards," he wrote. "Perhaps while State Superintendent I made too much of standardization."

The History of Missouri, third edition, by Duane G. Meyer (Springfield: Emden Press, 1993). Originally published in 1962 and previously revised in 1970, this is a comprehensive, readable, and generously illustrated history of Missouri.

History of the Ozarks, by Eunice Pennington (Point Lookout, Mo.: School of the Ozarks Press, 1971).

A History of the Pioneer Families of Missouri, by William S. Bryan and Robert Rose (St. Louis: Bryan, Brand and Co., 1876).

James Milton Turner and the Promise of America, by Gary R. Kremer (Columbia: University of Missouri Press, 1991), discusses Turner's work with the Freedmen's Bureau and the State Department of Education to establish schools for black children throughout the state.

Missouri Reader, edited by Frank Luther Mott (Columbia: University of Missouri Press, 1964), an anthology of writings about Missouri by Missourians, provides a rich and varied view of Missouri's cultural, political, and social history. The selections relating to education include "Missouri Rural Schools in the 'Eighties," by H. J. Blanton from his book *When I Was a Boy,* and "The Box Supper," by Joseph Nelson, from *Backwoods Teacher.* Other selections with information on education or the lack of education in Missouri include "Recollections of Early St. Louis," by Jesse Benton Frémont, and Jack Conroy's "Boyhood in a Coal Town," in which he recalls the joy of receiving the *Indianapolis News* and devouring it "from the front page to the last editorial, even the advertisements."

Missouri's Black Heritage, revised edition, by Lorenzo J. Greene, Gary R. Kremer, and Antonio F. Holland (Columbia: University of Missouri Press, 1993), originally published in 1980, draws on many documents and other sources to explore the black experience in Missouri.

The Old Country School: The Story of Rural Education in the Middle West, by Wayne Edison Fuller (Chicago: University of Chicago Press, 1982), reviews the development of schools in some midwestern states from early schools for farm children to consolidation. Progress in Missouri is mentioned throughout.

One-Room Schools of the Middle West: An Illustrated History, by Wayne Fuller (Lawrence: University Press of Kansas, 1994).

County histories of schools published by local groups, individuals, and historical societies proved to be especially helpful in my research for this book. A few of these references are:

The Era of the One-Room Rural Schools of Cedar County, Missouri, compiled and written by Jean Nipps Swain (privately published, 1988).

History of Clinton County, Missouri, by the Clinton County Bicentennial Committee (privately published, 1977).

History of Lafayette County Missouri Rural Schools, compiled and created by members and friends of the Lafayette County Historical Society (Concordia: The Concordian, 1996).

The History of Rural Schools of Putnam County, 1843–1965, compiled and written by the Putnam County Historical Society (Milan: Milan Standard, 1986).

Readin' 'Ritin and 'Rithmetic, 1840–1981, compiled and published by Clarence R. Keathley and the Officers and Board of Directors of the Iron County Historical Society (Ironton, 1981).

Rural Schools of Dallas County, Vol. 1, compiled by Thelma E. Kurtz (Buffalo: Dallas County Historical Society, 1992).

Sketches of Wright County, part three, *Schools and Education*, compiled and written by Vearl Rowe (privately published).

Index

Numbers in bold refer to illustrations; for specific schools, check references for the appropriate county or town

About the Author

Sue Thomas, a former elementary school teacher, is a freelance writer whose other books include *The Poetry Pad, Curtain I, Curtain II,* and the historical fiction novel for preteens *Secesh.* She lives in Kansas City.